UNBROKEN

SEVEN STORIES OF LIFE CHANGE
FROM THE OZARKS

TABLE OF CONTENTS

DEDICATION

We dedicate this book to all who've been broken.
May this book help you find the tools
to become like new again.

The book you are about to read
is a compilation of authentic life stories.
The facts are true, and the events are real.
These storytellers have dealt with crisis, tragedy, abuse
and neglect and have shared their most private moments,
mess-ups and hang-ups in order for others to learn and
grow from them. In order to protect the identities of those
involved in their pasts, the names and details of some
storytellers have been withheld or changed.

INTRODUCTION

Have you ever felt broken? Maybe you struggle with addiction, suffer the pain of abuse or are deeply affected by broken relationships.

In the middle of pain and desperation, we can end up wondering, *Will this ever end? Is happiness even possible? Is this all there is to life?*

This book contains seven true stories from real people right here in the Ozarks who overcame seemingly insurmountable obstacles — and who learned to take the shattered pieces of their lives and create something new and beautiful.

So if your struggles leave you wondering if there is any hope for you, our answer is an emphatic, "YES! Life change is possible! Even for us! Even for you!"

As you read these exciting stories of some crazy life experiences, expect to be inspired. You'll learn how men and women just like you found the secret to living an amazing life filled with purpose. May their stories encourage you to do the same.

WANTED

THE STORY OF JASON
WRITTEN BY MARTY MINCHIN

The Gulf of Mexico spread out before me as I shifted the captain's wheel a little too hard to the left, just to see what it would do.

The man they called Brick clapped me on the shoulder, noticing the move.

"It's okay, boy," he guffawed deeply and took a long drink of the Corona in his other hand. "There's nothin' out here you can hit."

I was 5 years old piloting a million dollar sailboat, and no one seemed to care.

When an enormous platform supported by four wide concrete legs came into view, Brick nudged me out of the way with his sturdy frame. "Run along now, son. We're going to circle up by that oil rig."

I scampered off the bridge and onto the deck, careful not to accidentally step on an arm or leg of a topless, sunbathing woman. They were scattered around like sleeping Barbie dolls, my mom among them with her wavy brown hair spread out under her head.

"Hey, Mom, I'm going to get in when the boat stops."

She opened one eye and then closed it. "Umm-hmm. That's fine, honey." The hot sun and an afternoon of cocaine and beer had made her agreeable to anything.

Like an Old West wagon train, the boats pulled bow to stern into a ring, creating a saltwater swimming pool in the middle. I pulled off my T-shirt and jumped into the water, glad for the waves lapping against my face that momentarily washed away the sights and sounds of the adult world I'd left on the deck.

ॐ ॐ ॐ

My mom brought me to Galveston, Texas, from Nevada soon after I was born. She'd partied hard since she was 12, and her cheerleader looks created a gravitational pull that men could barely resist. She'd met my dad at the skating rink, but he was long gone before I was born. My mom found herself the girlfriend of a series of powerful drug runners. She and I moved to the Gulf Coast with Dex, her latest boyfriend and a member of the powerful Bandido motorcycle gang. That made her an honorary "Bandido babe," a prized, off-limits trophy often found perched on the back of a motorcycle or snorting cocaine in the bedroom.

Our house, which sat high on 24-foot stilts, overlooked the beach on one side and a canal on the other. The coastal location was a convenient drop point for boats loaded with cocaine coming from Mexico. Dex distributed a lot of it to his network of sellers, but he kept enough at the house to fuel never-ending parties. People cycled through the house day and night, thugs, bikers and their women. They got in fights, tore stuff up, did drugs, drank and smoked.

WANTED

If the weather was nice, Dex herded the party out onto his sailboat — one of the largest in Texas at the time — and took the crew to sea. My world felt like a scene out of *Scarface*, with bricks of cocaine sitting around like knickknacks. My mom tried to keep me out of their bedroom, but I snuck in once and saw an impressive mountain of cocaine on her dresser.

The life of a young son of the girlfriend of a drug lord could be good. Along with the freedom and regular boat outings, I got great gifts. I got a Daisy BB gun for my 5th birthday, which was fun for one day. Then I shot the little girl next door in the cheek when I was supposed to be shooting cans from the deck of the house, and Dex snapped the gun in half over his knee. I was the first kid in the neighborhood to have a Big Wheel with water guns connected to it. Before I started elementary school, Mom and Dex gave me my own American Quarter Horse, which followed me around like a puppy when I visited it at the stable.

The ebb and flow of our life depended on Mom's boyfriends. When she and Dex broke up, we moved back to Nevada. We got an apartment in the town where my grandparents lived, but I might as well have just moved in with them.

పపప

As soon as Mom shut the bathroom door, I tiptoed over to where she'd left her purse. The bag's wide opening gave me an easy view of the contents. I stuck my hand in and sifted through the receipts, coins and candy wrappers. It only took a few seconds to find what I was looking for: a small plastic baggie.

I pulled it out of the purse and held it up toward the window. Yep. Just what I thought. It was filled with tiny dried greenish-brown leaves.

Weed.

"Grandpa!"

It was the 1980s, and I'd gotten an earful of Just Say No and D.A.R.E. at school. I was determined to rat my mom out. *Do a good deed and kill the weed.* How many times had I seen her passing a joint around with her friends in our living room and she said they were smoking cigarettes? I wasn't stupid.

Grandpa met me in the hallway outside the bathroom. I held up my prize.

"Mom's doing drugs, Grandpa," I said, smiling triumphantly. "I found this in her purse."

He snatched the bag from me and stamped into the bathroom that Mom had just vacated.

"Dad, don't you dare!" Mom shoved her long hair over her shoulder and grabbed at the bag. "That's my private property!"

"Jason found it in your purse, Debbie. I told you not to bring drugs into this house."

Grandpa opened the bag and tipped the contents into the toilet. The weed floated on the surface of the water before he flushed.

"You little snoop!" Mom screamed, slapping me on the cheek, then the arm. Her eyes blazed when she looked me in the face. "What were you doing in my purse?"

She raised her arm again, and Grandpa grabbed it, pulling her out of the bathroom.

"Debbie, I have told you a hundred times to keep your personal life personal. No drugs in my house. Do you hear me?"

She glared back at him.

"Now, go get your purse, and get on out of here. Jason can stay with us for a few days until you calm down."

Grandpa placed his hand firmly on Mom's back and ushered her out the front door. Weeks went by before I saw her again.

అఅఅ

Life with my grandparents wasn't bad, although I couldn't help longing for my mom to come get me. She was my mom, and I loved her, no matter how messed up she seemed.

The days at Grandma and Grandpa's were filled with chores. There were peacocks and pigs, horses and chickens, and everything had to be fed and watered daily. I worked around the farm before and after school and sometimes into the evening.

Mom occasionally took me back to our apartment, but she inevitably had a party to go to, and I ended up back at Grandma and Grandpa's. She'd show up every so often, usually with a new guy and a gift to keep me happy. I got the cool sweatpants with pockets on the knees and a Top Gun flight jacket.

By the time I was in fifth grade, Mom was partying every night. Her party friends in those days included a road crew she'd met at a bar. She told us that one night a guy broke into her apartment and attacked her, and she knew it was a guy from the road crew because she saw the reflectors on his jacket. She went to the hospital, and tests there confirmed that she'd been raped. Too traumatized to stay in town, she dropped me off with my grandparents and moved to Colorado to stay at her younger sister's dairy farm. When I finished the school year, she picked me up — with her new boyfriend — and took me back to Colorado.

ॐॐॐ

"Jason, wake up!"

I forced my eyes open and looked out my bedroom window. The sky was black.

"Geez, Mom, what are you doing? What time is it?"

As my vision came into focus, I saw a huge grin on her face.

"We're going shopping!" She waved what looked like a check in front of my eyes.

The digital clock in the car read 3 a.m. when I settled into the front seat, my mom babbling about the clothes and shoes and video games she was going to buy me. We pulled into the 24-hour store, which was like an enormous Kmart combined with a county fair. Along with racks of anything you'd want to buy, there was a theater, a kiddie roller coaster and power swings.

"Mom, how are we going to afford this?" Without a Bandido boyfriend, Mom was forced to take a rent-subsidized apartment in the projects, where I'd succeeded in getting into a fight almost every day with the rough kids who lived there. Mom hadn't worked full time since she'd gotten in a terrible motorcycle accident when I was a toddler.

She leaned over and whispered in my ear, trying to contain her excitement.

"Do you see this check?" She held it up again. "Two thousand dollars. Can you believe it?"

Mom practically danced into the store, pulling out a shopping cart and heading for the children's clothes. Thirty minutes later, it was full of everything a sixth-grade boy could want.

Apparently, we had money to spare, and Denver had several stores that stayed open all night. Mom loaded our purchases into the trunk, and we were off to the next stop on our pre-dawn shopping spree.

ॐॐॐ

At one point, Mom had attended nursing school. In Colorado, she found a job working for Danny, a young man on dialysis who'd already had three kidney transplants. He was the same age as Mom, and he paid her to cook and clean house for him. Danny was like the scrawny, funny high school nerd who could never land the pretty girl. But he possessed the magical power of weed. He and Mom were an odd pairing, but their working relationship quickly turned personal.

To earn a living, Danny sold marijuana in large quantities. There was so much weed in his apartment that if you swept the floor you'd probably pick up a quarter pound of it. After he skipped dialysis a few times because my mom couldn't take him, he almost died. So he moved into our apartment and brought his business with him. Once a week, a pair of Mexican guys showed up at our doorstep, and each dropped off a trash bag full of marijuana.

The bags of weed came in pounds of round and square bricks, where the leaves had been pressed into the shape of a Tupperware container. Given Danny's questionable health combined with his hard partying, Mom took over the drug business and became the neighborhood weed lady. She stashed the bags of marijuana in her closet and sold to customers who came to our door. If Mom wasn't home, I let the regulars in, and they got their stash out of the closet and left payment on her dresser.

Soon, I began to help myself to her inventory. She had so much marijuana in her closet, she never noticed I'd slip a brick into my backpack each Monday morning. She partied every night, and she'd only drag herself out of bed long enough on school mornings to wake me up. She was sound asleep when I snuck into her and Danny's room. It's not that I needed the money, and I didn't want to smoke the weed myself. I wanted to be cool.

I became the middle school go-to guy for weed. I sold it out of my backpack for $5 a pinch, and there wasn't a day that I didn't get on the school bus to go home with less than $100 in my pocket. I kept my bills neat, all facing the same way, organized from smallest denomination to largest and folded in half, just liked I'd seen the guys do when selling crack in front of my building. I may not have been the most popular kid in school, but all of the jocks, preps and cheerleaders brought their lunch money to me.

I preferred to hang out with the tough kids. I was the only white kid in the projects, and my homies were teenage drug dealers, gang members and thugs. We'd skip school and take the bus downtown, and I never lacked money to shop at the mall. I loaded up on hats, sunglasses and bandanas, skates and skate covers. I owned every new pair of Reeboks and gangster Nikes that came on the market. Mom never asked me where I got all of the stuff.

ৡ৵ৡ৵ৡ৵

Derek took a long pull on the joint and handed it to me. I leaned back against my bed and closed my eyes, ready to take a hit myself. It hadn't taken long for me to become a seller *and* a smoker of marijuana.

"Jason?" Mom's voice was right outside the door. "What are you guys up to?"

"Uh …" I looked at the doobie in my hand and threw it across the room. A tiny stream of smoke drifted above the carpet where it landed.

"Just hangin' out, Mom. Nothing much."

Mom stuck her head in the door and glanced around. We plastered innocent looks on our faces and forced smiles.

"We're just talking, Ms. D.," Derek chimed in.

Mom sniffed the air. "Jason, are you smoking pot?"

I didn't have time to answer before she spotted the smoldering joint.

"Are you kidding me?" Mom's voice came out as a high-pitched squeak. "You kids better get that out of there before you burn this apartment down!"

I gingerly lifted the joint out of the carpet.

"You know what? Both of you. In the living room with me, now."

We followed Mom to the sofa, and she pulled out another joint.

"You want to smoke weed? Then smoke."

We smoked, and smoked, and smoked, while Mom glared at us. We smoked until we were sick and on the verge of freaking out.

Mom's parenting effort, however, didn't work. She smoked so much weed and left so much of it around the house that she couldn't make a convincing case that smoking it was wrong. She conceded and allowed me to smoke it in the apartment but forbade me to take it out the door. She became the "cool mom" in our building, and soon she'd sit around and smoke marijuana in the living room with my friends and me. She had the best weed around, and our apartment was filled with joints, bongs, pipes and any other paraphernalia needed to smoke.

When I turned 14, my birthday present was waiting for me when I came home from playing pool after school.

"Mom, what the heck is that?" An elongated, lantern-like device stood in the middle of the room.

"Come here, I'll show you."

Mom opened one of the glass doors, and inside were the marijuana plants I thought I'd hidden in my room.

"These will grow a lot better in here," Mom said. "You won't be able to grow a lot of plants in it, but it will be a nice personal supply. Here's the switch. Try turning it on."

The hydroponic grow box lit up inside, providing the same light and nourishment for my plants they'd get outside.

"I traded some weed for it," Mom said proudly.

We found an out-of-the-way place for it in the living room, and the mirrors on the outside of the doors disguised the tiny garden inside.

❦❦❦

It was only a matter of time before I went to jail, a rite of passage that for me marked another milestone on the road to becoming a man. Every move I made was a baby step toward the prison door.

Everyone I knew had been to prison. The older kids I

hung out with in the projects were in and out of jail, as were Mom's friends. Mom and Danny were picked up once — along with 10 and a half pounds of weed and an assault rifle — when the police raided our apartment.

The drug scene I operated in was profitable, but it was littered with casualties. Friends went to prison and died for drugs. Junkies I knew spent their lives finding a way to pay for their next hit. There was plenty of gore in the drug world, but I saw more of the glory.

I wasn't scared of jail, but I tried to stay a step ahead of the police.

༺༺༺

The night Mom and Danny got out of jail, the Mexicans arrived at our door to resupply the weed the cops had taken. Mom and Danny decided it was time to move, and they had enough money to buy a five-bedroom house in the suburbs. Derek, my friend from across the hall, was going to move in with us, and he and I chose blue carpet for the basement where our rooms were. The high life was back. For my birthday that year, they gave me a white 1967 Mustang with black interior, even though I was several years away from eligibility for a driver's license.

Derek was 17 and didn't go to school. He had a full-time job selling crack, and he'd leave the house when I left for school and come home around dark. He taught me how to weigh and sell the white rocks.

Some friends and I went in the front door of school

one day and ran right out the back, meeting up later with Derek at an abandoned house. Whoever had lived there left a box of plates and breakable kitchen items in the garage.

Derek picked up a plate and threw it against the wall. It made a crashing sound as the pieces rained to the floor.

There was something intoxicating about boredom and breaking things and being teenagers. We smashed plates onto the floor and the sides of the garage, creating terrific sounds as the pottery cracked and shattered.

We emptied the box as quickly as kids disposing of an ice chest full of water balloons, and we wanted more. More breaking, more noise, more of the intense satisfaction of shattering something into a million pieces.

"Let's walk," Derek suggested, and we left the piles of pottery pieces and strolled through the neighborhood.

"I don't think that guy's home." Derek pointed at a house a few streets later. "Let's see what he's got in his garage."

We jimmied our way in a side window, sliding into a smorgasbord of stuff just waiting to be torn up.

No one really spoke. If it could be broken, we broke it. We dumped paint on the floor and kicked in old windows the guy had lying around. We threw his tools at the wall and bent the spokes of his bicycle wheels.

ॐ ॐ ॐ

"I'm sorry." My lip quivered as I stared up at the tiny camera in the corner of the cell. "I'll never do it again. I promise. I'll never cut school, and I'll be good."

I cried like a 3-year-old, the tears washing away my tough-guy façade. Someone in the police station had to be watching these surveillance cameras.

I stood on my toes to get closer to the lens.

"I'm so stupid. I don't know what we were thinking. I am really, really sorry. Can you call my mom? Do you know how long I'll be in here?"

I stared back at the solid metal door that clanked closed behind me after the officer took off my handcuffs and shoved me in the cell.

My mom is going to kill me.

The cops had caught us mid-vandalism spree, loaded us in their patrol cars and ushered us into the police station. "You boys are going to be in here for a long time," they told us.

My concrete block cell had a bunk, a toilet and the camera. When the door shut, the cell seemed to fill with cold air.

Will they ever let me out?

࿊࿊࿊

I got off easy that time. The guy who owned the house didn't press charges, and the cops seemed to think that calling our parents was punishment enough.

WANTED

"Do you see that?"

My friends and I rolled down the street in my buddy's dad's car, which we'd stolen out of his garage a few hours before. Nothing felt like freedom more than driving around town wherever we wanted.

"What are you talking about? That low-rider up there?" My friend in the front seat pointed to a kid riding a hot bike.

"Yeah. I bet that thing cost $3,000." Wow, I wanted that bike. "Let's get it."

Wes pulled the car up beside the kid. It was dark, and up close I could tell how cool the bike was.

"Cut him off."

The car whipped around in front of the kid, who paused for a split second too long. I jumped out into the street.

"Take off your coat!" The kid, who had gotten off the bike, stared at me like a frightened puppy. "I said, take off your coat, and throw it on the ground. You get on the ground, too. Lie down!"

The kid flattened himself face down on the road, and I shoved the bike into the backseat of the car onto Raymond's lap. The back wheel didn't fit, so I left the car door open and climbed back into the passenger seat. "Don't move until you can't hear the car engine anymore," I yelled back at the kid.

We slowly drove down the street while Raymond tried

to keep the bike in the car. I glanced in the rearview mirror in time to see the kid hadn't listened to my order and had already taken off running into the woods.

"This is too slow." I turned to the backseat. "Raymond, get out of the car and ride it to Wes' house. We'll meet you there."

Raymond obediently pushed the bike out of the car and took off. It felt good to have power over these younger kids. If I said something, they listened.

๛๛๛

Hanging out with junior high kids had its downfalls, however. Raymond couldn't keep his mouth shut, and in a matter of days he'd bragged to a girl at school about what we'd done. The girl's brother was the kid we'd stolen the bike from, and within days the cops were at my house arresting me for armed robbery.

I did two years in juvy for stealing that bike and then another two years for breaking into a cop car and stealing an AR-15 semi-automatic rifle. I was 18 when I got out of jail for that arrest, having spent the majority of my teenage years behind bars. I'd completed seventh grade before I went in, skipped eighth grade by filling out some workbooks and made it 14 days into ninth grade before I got in trouble again.

Jail wasn't much of a teacher, at least of anything helpful. In juvy, I mostly learned how to be a better criminal. Juvenile prison can be as violent as adult prison, and my cellmates included a 14-year-old accused of stabbing someone to death and a guy charged with cutting a girl up so badly she died.

If I'd wanted to be reformed, there were programs for that in prison. I ran into a few guys who seemed to genuinely want to change their lives and stay out of trouble, but they were rare.

There was a church service in prison, but I didn't attend because that might send a message to the other inmates that I was weak. I did talk to God every time I got locked up and asked him to get me out of there.

Mostly I just woke up every morning thinking about how I could smuggle things into the institution to sell and make money. Life in jail was very similar to life on the streets — just more confined.

శార్ శార్ శార్

I walked out of prison a legal adult, and my uncle showed up to get me. He helped me get a 1985 Mustang, and he gave me some weed and a pager so I could get back into business.

I did try to get a real job. A large food supply company had an opening, and the interview was in its warehouse.

The application asked me to list my skills. I knew they were hiring forklift drivers, so I wrote that in, even though I'd never driven one before. I could drive boats, dirt bikes and tractors, so I figured a forklift couldn't be that difficult.

The supervisor let me watch him for about half an hour first. I paid close attention as he shifted levers and pedals to move the forklift around.

"Okay. Your turn." The supervisor climbed out of the driver's seat. "Hop in and move that pallet over there."

I settled into the seat and took a deep breath before driving the forklift over to the pallet. I looked rusty, but I got the job.

The pride my mom and grandparents felt in me finally doing something responsible was short-lived. The job paid $9 per hour, and I had to get up at 7 a.m. to make it to the warehouse in time for my shift. I had an image to uphold. My Mustang needed a paint job and a new interior, and I was used to having nicer things than I could afford on that pay.

I quit. Selling drugs would get me the cash I needed much quicker.

I reconnected with a girl I'd met at a rave when I was 14, and her Mexican boyfriend had a connection for cocaine. I'd limited my drug use to weed and wasn't into needles, but my new crowd pushed me to try shooting up.

Curiosity eventually got the best of me, and one night I injected myself with cocaine.

The effects were immediate. I got tunnel vision and collapsed on the couch thinking I would die. I didn't, but when I came to my right mind, all I could think of was, *I'll never do this again.*

That resolve lasted until the cocaine wore off. I was already addicted, and later that night I tried shooting up meth. Needles became my method of choice for ingesting drugs, and if I didn't get a fix when the previous one faded, I'd get sick.

❧❧❧

We loaded Lawson into a Ford Probe and drove him back to my apartment. I taped him to a chair and held him at gunpoint for three days. People came in and out of the apartment, but I knew they wouldn't say anything. This guy owed so many people money that if we didn't kill him, someone else probably would.

Lawson didn't owe me any money. A guy nicknamed Face said he'd give me some of the payout for the kidnapping. Otherwise, I didn't care. I made Lawson's life miserable for a few days, slapping him around if he tried to fall asleep. The consequences didn't cross my mind. I was just the muscle, doing my job.

❧❧❧

"What do you want?"

Face answered the door, and I could see the fear in his eyes already. He knew that he owed me money for taking Lawson hostage and that I needed to collect it. Cocaine and meth habits were expensive.

He pointed to the cordless phone he was talking into. *I'm on the phone,* he mouthed.

"That's okay," I said loudly. "I'll wait."

I rifled through Face's entertainment center, pulling out CDs and video games for closer inspection.

Face motioned for me to stop.

"I'm just looking at stuff. Finish your phone call."

Face finally hung up the phone, then looked pointedly at me as I sat in the recliner. I knew Face kept a pistol hidden in there.

"Look, I need that money today. You owe me $300."

"I ain't got no money. I told you."

L.A., Face's girlfriend, walked out of the bedroom at that perfectly timed moment with a large envelope with RENT written on it.

"I'll take that." L.A. handed me the envelope, and I took out three $100 bills.

I glared at Face.

He looked scared. "I ain't got no dope!"

I picked up a bag on the coffee table and pulled out a coin purse. Inside was a roll of $100 bills.

I was suddenly furious that Face had lied to me, and he had to pay.

"For that lie, I'm taking everything you have. You told me you didn't have anything!"

৵৵৵

The cornfields of the Midwest flashed by my window on the Greyhound bus, and I was thankful to be anywhere but Colorado. My cousins and I had run from the cops the night before after I shot at a guy and his girlfriend in a parking lot with a sawed-off shotgun. I'd hit the guy a few times with what probably amounted to birdshot, but they were after me for assault with a deadly weapon.

I'd spent the previous evening high and freaking out on the floor of a friend's apartment after the cops pulled my buddy out of the nearby laundry building and arrested him. The cops patrolled the apartment complex and towed my car.

My roommate Alex arrived that night to pick me up. I threw on sweatpants, a Dallas Cowboys starter coat and a long blond wig before running outside and jumping in Alex's van. I called Grandpa, who had a standby bus ticket waiting for me at the station. I got on the 11 p.m. bus.

I didn't want to move back in with my grandparents, so I took an uncle's offer to move in with him and his family at an Indian reservation in Wyoming. We picked up an ounce of meth on the way, and when we got there, I got a job making $75 per day pulling transmissions out of junked cars. I had a little money in my pocket, and I felt safe on the reservation.

Drinking and smoking weed were popular pastimes there. I met up with a friend one night, and I stopped at a gas station to pick up alcohol on the way to pick up my girlfriend from the movie theater. I ran into a guy I'd gotten in a fight with several times before, and the last time he'd broken my nose. His name was Darren.

"Let's get out of here," I told Stella as soon as she was out.

I watched Darren and his friends pull up behind us,

and their headlights stayed on my tail all the way to Stella's house. They stopped when I stopped, and Darren jumped out and walked up to my side of the car.

When he leaned his head toward my open window, I pulled out a knife and stabbed him in the neck. As he crumpled onto the street, I peeled out toward my uncle's house.

Within minutes, my game was up. The cops blocked off the street, and I could hear the police dogs barking outside.

I'd have tried hiding under a hidden door in the hallway floor that provided access under the house, but I knew the dogs would find me there.

"Stella, tell the cops I'll come out. But tell them I want to tell you goodbye first."

I was on the run for shooting a guy, and I might have killed Darren. I knew I could be going away for a long, long time.

The cops took me to jail. Darren was alive, and he showed up in court with his parents. I hung my head, knowing I had no real defense.

Darren's voice startled me back to reality when he interrupted the judge.

"Your Honor, can I say something?"

"Okay."

"Jason and I have a history. We've gotten in a couple of fights, and I hurt him pretty badly one time when me and my buddies jumped him. When Jason stabbed me, he was doing it in self-defense."

WANTED

What?

My mouth almost fell open at this unexpected reprieve. *Was Darren actually asking the judge to let me off? Was I going to walk away from stabbing a guy scot-free?*

The law was not on my side, however. There was no self-defense clause, and the judge sentenced me to about two years and extradited me back to Colorado. Soon after the cops transported me from the bus station to the jail, Mom came to post bond, and I got out.

࿇ ࿇ ࿇

Mom never liked me having girlfriends. I was her only child, and she wanted to be the only woman in my life. I met Wanda in Denver, and when she and Mom got into a huge fight, I moved out of Mom's apartment. I tried to be responsible and got a job driving a forklift for $14 per hour, but the cops showed up there on my second day and arrested me on what later were determined to be trumped-up charges that my mom had filed.

Wanda's parents, who had money, hired a lawyer for me and bonded me out of jail. I asked Wanda to marry me, and we went to the courthouse to tie the knot.

We were 19 and 20 years old, and both of us found decent jobs in Denver. But the lure of drug money remained strong, and we soon quit to sell meth and weed full time. We bought a house outside the city, paid cash for cars and got a pit bull puppy. We got high all of the time.

Sometimes it was difficult to separate reality from paranoia, but less than a year after we moved in, I was sure that someone was watching our house. Our across-the-street neighbors were on vacation, but someone was sitting on their front porch in the dark.

"Wanda, go upstairs." I kept my voice calm. "Flush everything, then get the car keys and the dog. When I back out of the driveway, you run outside and jump in the car with me."

The chase through the still night seemed almost surreal. The cops didn't turn on their lights, and the open roads were almost empty. We drove more than 20 miles before the car ran out of gas, so we pulled into a 7-Eleven and hustled inside.

Mom and her boyfriend cleaned out the evidence from our house while we drove, but the cops put me in jail for violating the conditions of my bond. I served my time, and three days after they released me, I had a needle back in my arm.

🍃🍃🍃

"Hey — I'm going to stop by the bathroom before we head out." Wanda nodded and pushed the cart toward the cash register. We had moved into a motel in Denver and needed to pick up a few things at Kmart.

As soon as Wanda was out of sight, I cut a path around the outer edge of the store to the sliding glass door out to the parking lot. My cousin was waiting, just as we planned.

WANTED

I was abandoning ship.

Wanda and I were addicted to heroin, and I could see no end to it. We had gone from living in our dream house with everything we wanted to robbing and stealing daily to feed our addiction.

When I went in gas stations, I would see young kids and babies, and I wanted to feel like they did, like I was normal again. I knew that would never happen if I stayed with Wanda.

My cell phone buzzed 15 minutes later.

"Where are you? I've been at the checkout waiting."

No need to mince words. I was already gone.

"This isn't going to work. I'm sorry, Wanda. We're done. I'm heading out of town."

I needed help to kick my addiction. I knew I could turn to my mom — who hated Wanda. I knew my mom would do anything to have me back. Instead, I called my grandfather, who'd moved from Nevada to Missouri. My grandfather sent me money and a bus ticket to join him in Missouri.

෴෴෴

Soon after I arrived in Missouri, I was doing meth and ended up in the Cedar County Jail for a probation violation and a dirty urine analysis. They stuffed me in an 11-bunk cell with 24 other people. Thirteen guys had to sleep on the floor. The weakest guy in the group had to sleep next to the toilet.

The living conditions were horrible, and no one, not even criminals, should have to stay in a place like that.

I had to get out.

"Hey, guys, let's tear this place up so they have to let us go."

No one argued with that suggestion.

I broke the shower drain with a broomstick. The jail was over the county courthouse, and below the three-inch drain was an open space above the drop ceiling below us.

Like a bunch of witches making a brew, we stuffed the shower drain full of every flammable item we could find. In went newspaper, toilet paper and T-shirts. We finished with a long fuse made of rolled newspaper.

"Light it!"

The flame traveled down the newspaper, and our floor and the courthouse ceiling were soon burning.

It was Sunday afternoon, but the sheriff's office was next door and responded immediately to the 911 call.

By the next day, 20 of the 24 guys in the jail were gone — the four of us remaining were the ones they thought had set the fire. The others were shipped to a different county or let out on bond, and it wasn't long before we were released as well. My probation officer told me that as long as I didn't catch any new felonies, I was good.

I felt like a free man. When my girlfriend was seven and a half months pregnant with my first child, I got a job at a construction site. That could have been the start of a new life, but that would have been like walking on eggshells with combat boots. I still had a long list of charges against me in more than one state, and one run-in with the law could send me back to jail.

❧ ❧ ❧

The car slid quietly across the interstate, the combination of black ice and high speed propelling Karen and me across the median into oncoming traffic.

"Lean back!" I grabbed Karen by the neck and shoved her back against the driver's seat so that I could lean over and take the wheel. We spun out of control at 90 miles per hour and went through a median, three lanes of traffic and a barbed-wire fence before we stopped in a field.

Karen slumped forward, grabbing her belly.

"Contractions," she said quietly.

She'd hit her stomach on the steering wheel. The baby wasn't due for another six weeks.

I got her out of the car, and we walked back to the road and flagged down a car. An older couple stopped and called 911 while I sat with Karen. I just wanted her to be okay. I drove the car through a ravine and back onto the shoulder of the road so Karen would have somewhere to sit while we waited for the highway patrol.

She started bleeding, and the contractions worsened.

"It's okay, it's okay." I stroked her hair, trying to calm her down and keep my own panic in check.

A helicopter flew Karen to the hospital, and the older couple sent Karen's purse and our car keys with her. When I got in the car to drive home, I had no way to turn it on.

"Hey — just jump in," the highway patrolman offered. "I'll drive you to the gas station at the exit, and you can call someone to come pick you up."

"Sure." I easily accepted the offer.

"First I've just got to run you through my computer — standard procedure. What's your name?"

There was no running. As soon as my name popped up on his screen, he'd see that other police departments were looking for me.

I looked right at the officer.

"Wanted."

తతత

The baby lived thanks to medication that prolonged Karen's labor, and I served five years for second-degree arson. When I got out, I went on a nine-month crime binge. I racked up charges like a teenager on a shopping spree.

One time, I hid from cops under a pile of dirty clothes. Later, I got caught driving drunk. I led cops on a high-speed chase and then ran through a forest to evade them.

When I finally emerged from the woods, I faced a ring of cops, guns pointed.

I went back to jail and got out four months later.

I was almost 30 years old, and for the first time since I was 14, I didn't have to report to anyone. If I messed up again, though, I was looking at an automatic 15 years in jail.

It was time for real change. I wondered, for the first time in a long time, whether God could actually exist. The nine-month finale to my life of crime had been harrowing, and I'd escaped situations where I probably should have died.

I'd split with Karen, with whom I had two children, and gotten together with Lara, who had children of her own. She was a fellow junkie who I knew through friends.

We moved in together in a house we renovated, and we both got clean and sober through a 12-step program. We didn't want to get high anymore, and we didn't want to go to jail. I got a job, and she looked for one while volunteering at a senior center. We had a car. We started to live the life we wanted.

We still faced rough times, but things were changing. At one of our low points, Lara stopped by a food bank run by a church and got some information about a program that met on Wednesday nights that helped people overcome their addictions. We loved the program, and our kids loved the activities planned for them, too. The man who ran the program invited us to LifePoint Church, where he was the pastor.

Lara and I took the kids, even though I wasn't sure how the people there would react to me.

The people at LifePoint were not the types we were used to hanging out with. When we walked in, though, it was like the group opened their arms and gave us a hug. No one judged us. No one backed away.

It wasn't long before I wanted what these people had.

The pastor talked about God and Jesus and how Jesus died so that all people could be forgiven for everything they had done wrong.

I confessed to God, and I asked for forgiveness. I knew it was the right thing to do, but when I was baptized in front of the whole church to symbolize my decision to follow God, the experience rolled off me like the droplets of water in that pool. What I said I believed didn't sink in far enough to cause me to make any real changes in my daily life.

What Lara and I learned at church tended to stay at church. We didn't talk about the pastor's teaching at home, and we didn't read the Bible or talk to God in prayer. Eventually we just stopped going altogether. Then, Lara and I got in a huge fight, and the next day I had a moving van at the door.

ॐॐॐ

What am I doing?

I stood off to the side of the parking lot, which was filled with 59 guys about to board a bus.

They smiled and hugged each other, and occasionally a "Praise Jesus!" would float through the air. When the bus door opened, I slunk to the back and sat by myself. A few people tried to talk to me, but I was short with them.

We were headed to something called Men's Encounter, which a friend at LifePoint told me involved a lot of eating and crying and that I needed to go with an open mind and heart. He'd called or texted me daily for an entire week to remind me about it.

Our charter bus full of men joined another 450 guys at the church where the Men's Encounter weekend was held. The bigger group meant more clapping and hugging, and all I could think was I'd walked into some weird, crazy cult.

I took a seat in the auditorium and read over the checklist a volunteer had handed to me.

It was some kind of inventory of life issues. Pornography. Drugs. Adultery. Drinking. I was supposed to check off the ones I struggled with.

When we'd filled out the sheets, we divided into two lines in the aisles, each facing a giant wooden cross.

"Don't look at what your neighbor has checked off," the speaker in the front reminded us. "This is between you and God. When you get to the cross, pick up a nail and hammer your inventory to it."

Soft music played in the background, and I clutched my inventory in my hand. I had quite the checklist, and I was glad I could fold it in half so that no one else could see it.

When that nail sank into the wood, piercing a list of my wrongdoings, a sense of relief washed over me.

We gathered again the next night, and we sang some songs and talked to God together. A few guys went to the front and talked about how they had become followers of God and how God had changed their lives.

"Now, everyone line up again, and go back up to the

cross to get your inventory. Don't look at it until you get back to your seat."

I wasn't sure exactly which folded paper was mine, but I grabbed one where I thought I'd hammered the nail.

"Okay, now you can open them."

My page was blank.

"Everything you wrote on that paper? That was your baggage," the speaker continued. "It's what you were holding on to. Now you've given it to God. He's forgiven you, and you are as clean as that white piece of paper."

Before we left that weekend, those wooden crosses were covered again with men's "baggage," stuff they felt was causing them to do bad things and that they wanted to be free from. There were cans of chewing tobacco, cell phones, more paper with writing and even a laptop computer.

On our last morning, I looked out over the crowd. I was 35 years old, and my body showed evidence of hard living. I saw people who looked like me, and I saw guys who'd probably be walking into their law office on Monday morning. But we were all singing together, crying together and praying together.

I knew that I was changed. I could feel it. God had forgiven me for a life of wrongdoing, and I could go forward a different man.

෨෨෨

Something didn't feel right, though, about being placed in the "singles" group at the Men's Encounter, where I met with a few other single guys to talk about what we were learning over the weekend.

Technically, Lara and I said we were over, but I didn't feel single. When I sat with my group, I knew my heart and mind weren't open. In one small group meeting, I fell asleep.

I called Lara.

"I'm on this church weekend trip, and I'll be back on Sunday afternoon. We're going to get married Monday at the courthouse."

I'd proposed to Lara one Christmas Eve, but our engagement hadn't survived our latest fight. I told some of the guys at the men's weekend that I'd seen another girl in the few weeks Lara and I had been separated. They advised me to tell her and come clean, especially since the pastor had offered to marry us in the church. It would take a few days to get a marriage certificate.

Lara knew, though. When I got home, she looked me straight in the eye.

"You cheated on me, didn't you?"

I changed the subject. I made some jokes. But she knew.

She called me at 3 a.m. the next day, hurt and angry. That time, I didn't deny it. And I was miserable.

❧❧❧

I wallowed for several days, and I moved back to the town where Lara lived. Lara and I weren't done, and we made commitments to try and rebuild our lives. We married, and I applied for papers from the state so that I could start my own business.

It seemed awkward when I would pray with the kids, but I kept trying. Lara and I were clean and sober, and we faithfully went to church and to the addiction recovery program. I stopped by the church several days a week to talk to a pastor, and I got an app on my phone that sent me a daily Bible reading.

Sometimes, I've had to step away from situations that would have sent me into a rage when I was younger. I learned to take a deep breath and talk to God before reacting. By following God, I'm learning to become a better man. Lara and I don't live large, but I am thankful for a wife I love, an honest career, a decent place to live and a stable home for our kids.

I've been asked to go back to the Men's Encounter as a volunteer. They asked me to share my story of how God changed my life.

On the way out of church recently, a friend patted me on the shoulder.

"Jason, you're a blessing."

I looked down. "Okay, thanks."

It's hard to take a compliment, even the most sincere one. At LifePoint, however, with these people who love and follow God, I'm not an outcast.

I'm wanted.

FROM BETRAYAL TO BELONGING
THE STORY OF AUDRA
WRITTEN BY LAURA PAULUS

I missed all the warning signs.

Cheryl and I worked together at a travel station. We'd grown close after only a few weeks. She quickly filled the mom role for me, and I loved talking to her while we worked together at the travel station. We worked hard but made time to talk to each other, especially on breaks.

Supporting each other came easy for us. Cheryl listened to my problems and gave me advice. I listened as she told me about the grandchildren she'd been raising. I could not believe how much she gave unselfishly. I jumped in to help her provide her grandkids with Christmas gifts and other things they needed. We encouraged each other and helped each other out. We found kindred spirits in each other, and our friendship felt genuine, like a huge gift.

I guess that is why I failed to see her hidden self. I'd been thrilled to have someone who cared about me, and I missed the warning signs. I felt like I had a place to belong at that job with her on my side. And my naivety kept me from seeing the betrayal until too late.

I'd walked into work ready to start my shift. I had noticed the cop cars outside, but it did not raise any alarms since police often came through for the restroom or a drink while on patrol. Hurrying toward the back to put my purse in the office, I almost ran into the four officers walking out with Cheryl in handcuffs.

"Cheryl? What's going on?"

She looked at me and did not say anything.

"Cheryl. It's me. Tell me what happened."

One of the cops nudged her and said, "Let's go."

I turned and watched them walk out, wondering what mistake had occurred for my friend to be under arrest. I felt an arm on my shoulder and turned to see the remaining two officers standing there looking at me.

"Are you Audra?"

"Yes, I am. Why? What is going on?"

"We need you to come back to the office with us."

❧❧❧

I entered the world on a cold day in December. We lived in Denver, Colorado, for the first several years of my life. The label of Daddy's girl fit me perfectly as I loved spending time with him, and he adored me. As a chef, he loved to create amazing dishes he knew I would love. He also took me on father/daughter dates and brought me flowers. I felt supported and loved by him.

My brother Eli arrived shortly after I turned 3. I loved my baby brother and played the typical older sister role as I doted on him and spoke on his behalf. In fact, my parents worried my brother might be deaf since he never spoke. Eventually, after he turned 3, he surprised them with a flow of words while getting in trouble. He simply hadn't needed to talk before then. I did it for him.

My family moved to Arizona after a disagreement occurred between my dad and his brother, who pastored the church we attended in Denver. We moved away and did not have much of a relationship with any of my dad's relatives afterward.

While living in Arizona, my dad learned he had cancer. He appeared to be fine for a few months and then his illness became more evident. We moved to California where my dad continued to fight the cancer.

Unfortunately, the sickness spread throughout his body, and he passed away at the young age of 42, three days after my 6th birthday. Years later, I saw a picture of my dad near the end of his life. He looked like an 80-year-old man with his body shrunken in from the cancer.

When he died, I felt sad, but more than anything, my emotions consisted of anger and betrayal. *How could my dad die?*

Immediately after the funeral, my mother moved us to a small town in Missouri. I once saw a picture of my dad standing outside the church in our Missouri town as it was being built, so I know we had some type of connection with the town, but I was never sure why we moved there.

My mom and I were not close. I didn't feel a bond with her. It made me wonder if I had something wrong with me. She once told me she did not want children, and I had been an accident. This hurt me, especially considering that she seemed to be fond of my brother. Mom and I didn't fight much, we just didn't connect. She worked hard and did her best to raise us. She even took in her brother's daughter as her own.

My cousin Ashley, younger than me by four years, had been living in California with her mother in a shed infested with roaches and rats. She was learning to steal to survive. My mom refused to leave her niece in those conditions. Ashley came to live with us around the time I entered third grade. My widowed mom then had three children to care for on her own.

My grandmother on my mom's side also lived with us at times. Often sick, my grandmother required care, and my mother added one more person to her long list of responsibilities. To further complicate things, my grandmother favored Ashley over my brother and me. My mom attempted to even things out.

"Mother, you cannot only bring Ashley gifts when you come. Please bring all three kids presents or do not bring anything."

"Well, you all know Ashley and I are close. We share a special bond since our birthdays are almost the same day."

"I understand, but it is hard for Eli and Audra when you single out Ashley all of the time. You are their grandmother, too."

"Of course, I am. They know I love them."

I am not sure we did. We knew Ashley was the favorite, and she continued to be even after that talk. My brother and I did not feel we measured up in Grandma's eyes.

FROM BETRAYAL TO BELONGING

❧❧❧

We attended a very strict church and the school the church ran. Women only wore dresses or skirts, and those were extremely modest. The members in the church had strong ties to each other. Since people attended the church and the school, there seemed to be no reason to have friends or relationships outside of the congregation. This must have been a comfort to many. It provided a safe place for them to belong.

Which was fine, unless you did not feel like you belonged. The other women of the congregation stayed home, while the men worked. As a widow, my mom did not have the same option to stay home. She started going to school to become a nurse, and she also worked in order to support herself and us children. As a result, she had little in common with the other women.

I struggled to feel like I fit in as well. I still carried anger over losing my dad. I honestly felt most angry at God, although I dared not confide that to anyone I knew. I was pretty sure good girls weren't supposed to feel anger toward God.

❧❧❧

At the end of my fifth grade year in school, my mom scraped together enough money to buy a house in a nearby town. The added benefit of owning her home meant we no longer had to live in houses other church members owned. To our discomfort, the church checked in on us often at our previous house to see if we were following its rules. When we moved to our new house in Seneca, Missouri, we didn't go back to that church. In fact, we stopped attending church altogether.

Mom made sure we did our homework and got good grades while we were in elementary school. For a while, she continued to be rigid about making me wear skirts. But in seventh grade, I was allowed to wear pants. We also got a TV for the first time. Gradually, my mom let up on other things, too. She stopped paying attention to our grades. I started failing just to show I could, and she did not even seem to notice. It may have been due to her working long hours and simply being exhausted. Or maybe she'd stopped caring. It sure felt that way.

~~~

My mother married my stepdad the summer after I turned 16. Before the wedding, she asked me what I thought about it.

"Mom, I don't think you should marry him."

"You can't support me in anything, can you?"

"It isn't that. You haven't known him very long. He has four kids, Mom. They are not well-behaved." *He also does not treat you well, and you deserve better.* I did not share those thoughts with her, though, because that seemed too personal somehow. We were not ever vulnerable with each other.

"Well, I am marrying him, and you need to deal with it."

Our relationship really disintegrated at that point. My mom resented me for saying that she should not marry Jake. She did still lean on me to help. In fact, shortly after they married, Mom and Jake would leave me with the kids while they had "time away for a break," sometimes for a few hours, but many times for several days. One time, they were gone for two weeks. This left Eli and me with five young kids to care for with limited resources. We had little to no food. I often fed the younger kids rice and butter, while Eli and I ate spoonfuls of peanut butter — when we had it. We left the rice for the other kids since it seemed to fill their stomachs.

One time, we completely drained our propane tank, which heated our water tank and stove. My parents didn't have the money to buy more.

"Eli, can you supervise the kids while I heat up water in the microwave?"

"Why are you heating water?"

"These kids are filthy and need baths. I am going to heat up enough water to fill the tub. This is the only way I know how to do it."

There were no adults to help us. Our nearest neighbor lived more than a mile away. It seemed to fall on me to keep things going. And while I longed for Mom and Jake to step up and take care of us, things went smoother when they were gone. It stressed me out, but the kids were cared for, and I could manage them. As soon as our parents came back, things got chaotic.

Our home life would have continued on like this

indefinitely had David not shown up in my life. We met in school, and he started hanging around during the summer before 10th grade started. One time, when my parents were actually around, David came and took me to lunch since we had no food in our house. Mom freaked out that I was going out with a boy and kicked me out of the house. Just like that. What hurt most was getting cut off from my siblings. I cared about them and was pretty sure I knew how they'd be cared for in my absence. I had nowhere to go and no one except David. His parents decided to buy us a trailer from a neighbor, and we moved in and lived on love.

Love is all we had. We had no heat or air conditioning since we had no money. At one point during the height of summer, I had to go to the emergency room to be treated for heat exhaustion. We had little food and lived on bologna and cheese we kept in a cooler.

Life rapidly went downhill with David. He went from my knight to my nightmare. He drank a lot and could be very controlling. I'd dropped out of school and began smoking marijuana. I thought about trying to leave to find a better life, but David reminded me he would find me and drag me back. Besides, where would I go? I did not belong anywhere. So, I stayed and we partied. I started drinking in addition to smoking pot.

Someone reported me. The mention of a 16-year-old living in a rundown trailer caused the Department of Family Services (DFS) to show up and remove me. They wanted to return me to my mother, but I begged them not to. Others in the area spoke up and explained the living conditions there were not good. Mom and Jake somehow heard about it all and took off with the other kids before DFS could find them.

Initially, they placed me in a group home and then moved me to a nice foster home a few towns away. The family treated me well and had a daughter close to my age. Looking back, I regret not staying there. When David showed up for me, I went with him. In the system's records, I became an official runaway.

❧❧❧

David and I continued to party. I worked and supported both of us, but any time not spent working went to drinking and doing drugs. He became abusive, both verbally and physically. I felt worthless and depressed.

Eventually, I found a place to stay with a co-worker. She had kids, and I helped out with them in exchange for living with her. The situation worked well until her boyfriend and I were alone there. I barely got away from him, and the incident frightened me. I worried he would come after me if I told my friend, so I kept quiet. It ate at me, and my friend knew something must have happened.

"Audra, what is going on with you? You are quiet and don't seem like yourself."

"It's nothing. I am just tired."

"What's bothering you? You can talk to me. I am your friend, and I am here for you."

Maybe I should tell her. She is my friend. I would want to know if I were in her shoes.

I sat down on a chair and watched her folding clothes on the couch.

"Well, an incident happened to me last week. I have not said anything because I did not want to hurt you."

"You can tell me anything."

"Roger stopped by while you were at work the other day. The kids were napping, and I was on the couch reading. He came and sat next to me and started trying to kiss me. I pulled back, and he grabbed my arm and yanked me to him. I managed to pull my arm away —"

She jumped up quickly and got in my face. "How dare you sit here and make up things about my boyfriend. After all I have done for you. I should have known you would be jealous and try to pull this."

"What? I am not making this up. He came on to me."

"Pack your stuff, and get out of my house. Now."

୶୶୶

During this time, I worked with Cheryl, who'd been a bright spot in my life when I had so many bad things going on. That's why what I learned after her arrest felt like a personal betrayal.

Thankfully, the shock of seeing her escorted out of the store by police numbed my feelings. I walked back to the office with them in a daze.

Over the next several hours, the officers questioned me

as they showed me videos and gave me numerous examples of Cheryl's crimes. It turned out Cheryl had been stealing large amounts of expensive jewelry from the travel station's gift shop. I watched videos of her ringing up people for one item but handing them multiple bags to carry out.

As if this were not bad enough, much of the evidence made it look like I had been involved. I watched as the videos showed me covering the store while she ran out to her car for a minute. I'd thought she was grabbing a forgotten item. Instead, she'd been stashing merchandise. I even appeared in the video at times while she handed bags of jewelry to people. I was an oblivious 18-year-old kid. I had no clue what had been going on, but it did not look that way.

Eventually, they cleared me. They didn't have any solid evidence against me. I could tell by the way the police talked to me that they still thought I'd partnered with Cheryl. In a matter of a few weeks, I got fired for a minor offense. Clearly, the managers didn't entirely believe my innocence, either, and wanted to get rid of me.

෩෩෩

Without other options, I'd gone back to David. Eventually, he cheated on me, and I finally walked away from him. When I could, I spent the night on someone's couch. Occasionally, I slept in my car. I got a job at a Sonic Drive-in but spent most of my money on the substances that, once again, became part of my life.

UNBROKEN

My depression grew after I left David. Life went from bad to worse. Homeless, I found myself completely lost with no sense of direction. David had always told me what to do and how to think. Suddenly, I had all of this freedom, and it terrified me. I moved in with a girl I met who happened to be an alcoholic. We began to drink and do drugs together. We hung out with people who felt sorry for me.

One night, I felt hopeless. I had too much to drink, but I decided I did not care and wanted to keep drinking. I wanted to stop feeling life. My roommate left as I overdosed and stopped breathing. Somehow, a neighbor found me and performed CPR until the paramedics showed up. I survived despite suffering severe alcohol poisoning. It scared me so much that I gave up substances. For a while.

৵ ৵ ৵

I ended up moving in with David's sister during the summer almost a year after we had broken up. I had not seen him, and his sister rarely saw him much, either. I heard he'd moved in with his brother, who made him clean up his act and get a good job. This brought up feelings in me which caused me to get in touch with him. I wanted to forgive him and let go of the hurt I carried from our relationship. I felt it was important to do it in person.

"David, you hurt me. I need for you to know that. I also need you to know I forgive you."

"I know I hurt you. I was such a jerk. I never deserved you in my life."

I had not expected to hear that from him. I looked up at him and remembered how much I had loved him. *He really has changed. He is not at all the same jerk he used to be.*

We talked for several hours. We decided we did still love each other, and we wanted to be together. I moved in with him and gave it another chance.

Things were better between us — for a while. I'd been working at a Sonic Drive-in and made decent money. He worked, too, although I made more money. He did not mind spending my money and his. In November, I earned the opportunity to move to St. Louis and run a Sonic there. Due to the rigorous demands of the job, we decided David would stay behind while I went to St. Louis and got the job under control. He came a few weeks later. It irritated me to work every day for long hours and have no time to devote to him. Still, we did our best to make it work.

The following summer, David cheated on me again. He also changed our locks. I could not get in to get my stuff out of my own apartment. When I attempted to get in, he called the police on me. The time had come to be done with him forever.

❧ ❧ ❧

I went and lived with a friend from work. Jake and I did not know each other very well, but he appeared to be a nice guy. I needed a place to stay. It bothered me that he had the same name as my stepdad, but I pushed it out of my mind. We soon became romantically involved, and at the age of 23, I became pregnant.

I locked myself in the bathroom of a local department store as I took multiple pregnancy tests. Yep, positive every time. Stunned, I sank to the floor in the stall and tried to catch my breath. I had been told at a doctor's appointment that I would not be able to have kids, and I did not get pregnant while living with David despite years of unprotected sex. It seemed highly unlikely, and yet it happened.

Jake broke up with me and kicked me out shortly after finding out about the pregnancy. Around the same time, I lost my job at Sonic. Left with no job and no place to live on top of being with child, the hopelessness and devastation I felt shook me. Even in the worst of times, I had never lost my will to live. But pregnant and alone, I wanted to die. I begged God, who I had not prayed to in years, to take my life. I thought of ways to kill myself. And yet, I knew I could not do it. I could not kill myself or this baby. I had to face the consequences and deal with it all. I decided adoption would be the easiest way out of my mess.

Thankfully, a friend knew I needed to talk to someone wise. She invited me over to meet Anna, who welcomed me into her home and listened to me. She told me programs existed for unwed mothers, and she offered to let me live with her for a few weeks until we could find such a program.

࿐࿐࿐

In June, I loaded up my belongings, hugged Anna goodbye and moved to Lebanon, Missouri, to live at the Pregnancy Support Center (PSC). Nervously, I pulled up to the building and sat in my car for a minute. I noticed an older lady walking toward my car with a big smile on her face. I opened my car door and stepped out.

"Audra?"

"Yes?"

"Oh, I am happy to finally meet you after speaking on the phone the last several weeks. Welcome!"

"You must be Patty. It is nice to meet you."

Patty gave me a big hug and began grabbing my belongings out of the car. I quickly grabbed some things and attempted to keep up with this energetic woman.

"Okay, let me explain a few things. You can earn points by going to our Bible study, completing homework and attending classes. Then you can redeem these points for things you and your baby will need. We will take good care of both of you during your pregnancy as long as you work the program, too."

I settled right into life there. The staff and girls were very friendly. I got a job at a local diner to earn money. The center welcomed me with loving arms. The staff helped me to grieve through my choices, take responsibility for my actions and move forward with my life. This place became my refuge while I began to heal and learn more about the Lord. I began to learn God had plans for me and that he loved me. I felt at home right away, especially when I met Pam, another staff member who showed me unconditional love.

I also started attending a local church called LifePoint Church. The first time we went, I begged to sit in the balcony. Sitting down toward the front with Pam would indicate to all that I was a single, pregnant woman. I enjoyed the service and decided to come back the next time. The second time, Pam convinced me to sit with her where she usually sat.

It surprised me to find everyone welcoming and kind. Not one person made any rude comments about my condition as they tried to get to know me. It had been a long time since I had been in church, but not enough time to forget how my childhood experience differed.

తతత

At Pam's suggestion, I agreed to go away on a weekend retreat called Ashes to Beauty Encounter. We went with several women from LifePoint and churches all over Missouri. The weekend served as a time of healing for me. We heard stories from women who suffered lives filled with pain until God took it all away. Deeply moved by all I heard, I knew I wanted to give my life to Jesus, God's son who died for me. He could love me completely and would never betray me. I needed a relationship with him. So I prayed and invited him into my heart. In that moment, I *felt* God change my heart. I left the weekend with an unexplainable peace.

Accepting a relationship with Christ helped life to smooth out, but I still had no idea what to do about the baby. I found out the gender. My baby girl had about six weeks left before her due date. I needed a plan quickly. During those last weeks, I struggled to trust that God had a plan. But I clung to the promise in Jeremiah 29:11-13, which reads, "'For I know the plans I have for you,' declares the Lord, 'plans to prosper you and not to harm you, plans to give you a hope and a future. Then you will call on me and come and pray to me, and I will listen to you. You will seek me and find me when you seek me with all of your heart.'"

One day, I considered again all the pros and cons of keeping my baby. I wanted her. I even loved her, which really complicated it all. I had no idea how I would provide for this little girl. Even more, I feared I would not be a good mother to her. Motherhood wasn't modeled for me very well growing up. I also knew how it felt to grow up without a father. I did not want my daughter to face the same thing. Again, I asked God to open or close the door on my decision to keep the baby. The very next day, he seemed to provide the answer.

I worked a split shift at the diner. As I reached the end of the first chunk of my shift, I began thinking about the nap I had coming. I could hardly wait. Finished with all of my tasks, I walked or, more accurately, waddled over to my boss to let her know I would be back in a few hours.

"Actually, I need you to go back and help the cook finish the meal prep."

I went to the kitchen and began helping. It seemed pointless since the cook had prepped everything already. We talked for a few minutes and then I went back to my boss.

"Okay, Audra, I need you to wipe the salad bar down."

My boss had always been more than fair with me, and I liked her. But I grew frustrated at the way she acted determined to keep me at work when I wanted to be done. And when I reached the salad bar, still shining from the wipe-down I'd given it half an hour before, I decided I'd had enough.

"Molly, I don't mean to complain, but it seems like you keep giving me unnecessary stuff to do. I would love to go and rest before I have to come back."

"Audra, you are wrong. I have a very good reason for giving you meaningless tasks." She smiled at me and put her arm around my shoulder, pulling me to the side room we often used for parties. She opened the door and gave me a tiny push through as my brain registered the party. I looked around at the faces of my co-workers and then saw the pink decorations.

"Welcome to your baby shower!"

I could not believe it. I felt surrounded by loving support and presents — lots of presents. There were diapers, sippy cups, dresses, headbands and many other items a tiny human being might need. It took two carloads to get it all back to the center. The biggest gift that I got had to be when I realized God had answered my prayer. He provided all of the things I would need for me to keep my baby.

The ladies at LifePoint Church also threw me a huge shower, and they gave me more diapers and baby things. I could not believe the generosity of the women. The shower served as another reminder of how God would provide. I felt God washing away all of the fears and doubts holding me back from stepping up to the challenge of caring for my daughter. On top of that, the PSC told me and another pregnant girl, Janie, that we could stay until our babies were 1 year old.

Several weeks later, just short of my 24th birthday, I gave birth to my little girl, Cassie. For so long, I'd been scared I would be alone when I had my baby. But, again, God took care of me. Anna came for the birth, and Patty and Pam joined us. They had all provided emotional support through my pregnancy, and they continued to support me as I went through labor. And they were there when I got to meet Cassie for the first time.

I can't say life got easier because I made the decision to keep my daughter. I remained a single mom trying to get my life together and care for a newborn. The church and the PSC continued to support me and show me love.

In fact, the PSC designed a program, Project Thrive, specifically for Janie and me. This program provided transitional housing to allow us to live in a safe place while we attended school. It also enabled me to give up my job at the diner and begin caring for other children in my home. The money I earned babysitting made it possible for me to be a stay-at-home mom. Plus, I got to help other single moms as I watched their kids while they worked.

LifePoint continued to bless me and be a large part of our lives. When the water pump went out on my car, a man from the church bought new parts and made the repairs. He even replaced my cracked windshield and paid for my car inspection.

My daughter and I were surrounded by people who loved us. Pam and her husband became the parents I always wanted and the grandparents I thought Cassie would never have. And their daughters became my new sisters.

Next, I needed a godly man to share life with.

෯෯෯

I had seen Jake around during services and in the parking lot greeting guests. The way he looked at me told me of his interest. Pam knew him long before she knew me. After several conversations with him, she thought we would be good together. I knew I wanted a husband for me and a father for Cassie at some point, but I had no desire to rush into anything. I definitely did not want to rush into anything with a man who had the same name as two other men in my life who had hurt me. I could not help but think, *Three strikes, you're out!*

I attended another Ashes to Beauty Encounter weekend. God healed me further, which seemed odd as he had already done so much. Someone once told me God heals our emotional wounds like physical wounds. Sometimes old physical wounds need to be opened up to get the infection out. Only then can the wound heal properly. That is exactly what the process felt like. God and I kept digging deeper to pull out all of the infection. The weekend included some encouragement and a great time of ministry as well. I came back refreshed and ready to grow more.

A few days later, I saw Jake walking toward me. I quickly rushed tottering 16-month-old Cassie along as I tried to sneak out the door. To my embarrassment, Cassie grabbed Jake's hand as he came near, and the three of us walked hand-in-hand like a little family. Jake laughed as he interacted with Cassie. Then he looked over at me.

"Would you like to go on a date sometime?"

"Um …"

"Don't worry, I already spoke with Pam and her husband and asked them for permission. They agreed as long as you agree."

Who was this incredible man? Did he seriously ask my adopted parents if he could date me? This has to be the cutest thing to ever happen to me. How could I not go out with him?

"Jake, I'd love to go on a date with you."

And we have been together ever since.

❧❧❧

My spiritual journey has been amazing with LifePoint in the center. God has taught me the importance of forgiveness, both giving it and receiving it. While I do not have to forget what others have done to betray me, I no longer have to carry the hatred.

I realized that the people who betrayed me were imperfect and hurting, just like me. My broken relationships taught me to rely on Jesus, who can fulfill my needs. People are human and sometimes will let me down. And I will sometimes let them down. But God will never fail me.

I have forgiven my mom. I can only imagine how difficult life has been for her after losing my dad, raising three kids by herself and sharing a chaotic life with my stepdad. I would love to see our relationship repaired. Meanwhile, I'm thankful that God has given me positive influences in life, and I feel loved.

Part of learning about forgiveness meant contacting my brother Eli. Years after my mom kicked me out, he had gotten in touch with me and lived with David and me for a while. We had a heated disagreement, and I said some awful things to him. For a long time after that, we lost touch. After I sent him a letter asking for forgiveness, we began speaking again. In fact, he came to celebrate Cassie's 2nd birthday and Thanksgiving.

Jake asked me to marry him on Thanksgiving. Of course, I said yes. For the first time, I had a romantic relationship with healthy boundaries. We strive to honor God and each other. It feels like every detail has fallen into place as God must have intended it to be. He provided me with a home, loving people, a bright future and so much more.

I am learning to stop leaning on my own understanding and instead to lean on God. I have to trust him and allow him to be first, above all else. For too long, I carried shame and regret, tearing myself down in the process. I have learned, and am still learning, that God can change circumstances when I allow him to work in my heart. He loves me and will not let what I went through go to waste. I am not a mistake.

One of my favorite verses is Isaiah 43:18, which reads, "Forget about what's happened; don't keep going over old history. Be alert, be present. I'm about to do something brand new" (MSG).

I believe God chose me for a reason and with a purpose. He will not betray me. With him, I belong.

THE TROUBLE WITH HOME
THE STORY OF BRAYDEN
WRITTEN BY AMEERAH COLLINS

The hairs on my arm stood on end as I trudged through the woods. The cold metal of the pistol tucked in the waistband of my jeans pressed into my back. I glanced back at Mom's little house, distancing myself from the constant bickering and beatings her husband gave her.

To hell with it all, I told myself. *I can't stay here any longer. No one wants me, anyway.*

My worn sneakers kicked at the crunchy leaves as Mom's battered and bruised face entered my mind. The purple bruises against her hollowed cheeks. The blood trickling down her chin from her busted lip. The way her trembling hands wiped at her never-ending tears.

I can't be like him — like them. All the men who've hurt her. I can't grow up to be them.

Soon, I started weeping. I yanked the gun from my jeans, flipped it over in my hands, then pressed the muzzle to my temple. I felt weak as I pushed my other hand out to steady myself against a tree. I shuddered, sighed. My finger rubbed against the trigger.

Nobody will miss me. Why would they? The way my life is, nobody cares.

Aloud, I muttered, "They'll never care."

❧❧❧

I always believed my life began as a mistake. My parents never planned on having me. Mom got pregnant after partying, using drugs and alcohol and being irresponsible with my dad. During her pregnancy with me, they didn't change their wild ways. At a party, Mom started having contractions. Just hours later, she delivered me at a nearby clinic. Everything was so unplanned. From the very beginning, nothing was ever thought out.

When I was 9 months old, Mom left Dad. She said she didn't want me anymore. A few months later, Dad showed up at his parents' house with me in his arms. "Here, take him," Dad said. "I can't deal with Brayden anymore. He's too much for me." Just when my grandparents were about to adopt me, my parents got back together and took me back. We ended up moving around a lot. Trouble seemed to really hit home the year I turned 9 years old, though.

I sat up in bed, my flimsy covers falling to my lap. I frowned at the loud sounds coming from the living room. Harsh thuds, slaps, low grunts and shouts. Worrying for my mother, I scurried from beneath my sheets and hopped out of bed. Scuffling toward the living room, my eyes widened as the noises grew louder with each step. I turned the corner and gasped.

Mom. Dad's brother. Together. On the floor.

I whirled on my heels and raced back to my bedroom. I eased the door shut and dived back under my covers. My breathing grew ragged as I tried to erase the images from my mind. I couldn't believe Mom and my uncle were together *in that way*. I didn't understand how they both could do that to Dad. I sank deeper under the comforter and clamped my palms against my ears.

Just when I thought the sounds would never end, the front door creaked open, then slammed. Heavy footsteps stomped across the floor before abruptly stopping. Curses bellowed through the air. Mom screamed, and louder bangs and thuds rang out. It didn't take a genius to figure out my dad had returned home to see what I'd seen.

After that, Dad left, and life got hard. He still picked up me and my little sisters, Violet and Ella, to spend time with him, but he didn't live with us anymore. Mom partied nearly every night, brought home different men and left me in charge of my sisters. Getting food in the house proved to be tough. Many times, my grandparents, my dad's parents, brought food over and bought any school or household items we needed. Still, I usually only ate once a day. I tried to make sure my sisters and Mom had enough. If I had to settle for chips and ketchup for dinner, then I'd do it for them.

On school days, I made sure to wake before my sisters so I could dash into the living room and cover my mom's naked, passed-out body. I didn't want my sisters to see what she looked like after her typical nights of men, drugs and liquor. I tried to shield them from that side of her. I didn't want them to see Mom chasing her next high or no-good guy. After three years, my sisters and I moved in with Dad when I was 12 years old.

Every other Sunday, my grandparents picked us up to attend church with them. We usually spent the afternoon with a family from the church since Violet was good friends with their daughter. Plus, they had an older son who threw the football with me outside.

"C'mon, guys. Grandma will be here soon!" I shouted toward my little sisters' bedroom as I poured bowls of cereal and milk on the kitchen table. "You don't want to be late for church."

"We're coming, we're coming." Violet came into the kitchen with Ella skipping behind her. She rubbed her eyes and plopped onto the chair. "I hope we're going over to Shyanne's house after church. We always get to play there."

"And her mommy is so nice, too!" Ella added.

"Yeah." I grinned. "And Julius is usually down for a game of football or something."

After church that day, my grandparents allowed my sisters and me to go over to Shyanne's house just as we anticipated. As it grew later in the evening, it was determined we'd spend the night, and my grandparents would pick us up in the morning. While my sisters bunked with Shyanne, I slept in the room with Julius.

In the middle of the night, he edged closer to me in the bed. Suddenly, he wasn't the cool and easygoing guy who threw the football around or shot hoops with me. He seemed much older as he sidled beside me and his hand slowly crept toward me under the covers.

"Wh-wh-what are you doing?" I sputtered and scooted away, nearly falling off the bed.

"Calm down." Julius chuckled lightheartedly, but his brows were knitted. "I want to show you something. What I'm about to do is normal. People don't talk about it, but it's okay to do it."

"I don't … I don't want to do anything, though. I just want to sleep."

"It's all right, Brayden. Just don't say anything about it. We can sleep after."

Julius was always so nice to me and did more stuff with me than my father ever did. I didn't understand why he wanted to touch me under the comforter. I simply knew I didn't want to lose his friendship.

So just as he instructed, I didn't say anything about it — not to anyone. I continued going to church with my grandparents and sisters, and we continued spending nights at Shyanne's house.

I wanted to believe it was okay, what Julius had been doing, but as the Sundays passed, I became withdrawn, fearful and I didn't feel like myself anymore. I felt dirty, misused and confused. I thought about telling Dad, but I didn't want him to disown me after finding out. Each time I decided to tell a grownup what was happening, a nagging thought in the back of my head kept telling me no one would believe me.

So I stopped going to church with my grandparents. I began viewing people in church differently. If I could get hurt at the home of a well-known family at church, then I didn't want much to do with the church or even God. About a year later, Dad moved us to a new town. I still didn't mention what happened with Julius. I tried to let it go, but it haunted me.

He haunted me.

రిరిరి

During my early teenage years, Dad started using drugs and drinking alcohol more heavily than he ever had. Over the years, he'd become a big-time drug dealer and oftentimes took me on runs with him.

When I was just 16 years old, he introduced me to alcohol. I wasn't too against the idea of drinking. I knew it offered a sort of solace, and I had plenty of experiences in my past I wanted to forget. Like Julius. I needed to forget what he did.

"If you're gonna drink," Dad said as he slouched against the living room sofa with a glass pipe in his hand, flickering a lighter beneath it, "you're gonna do it right here with me, boy."

"Yeah, okay." I nodded. An aching feeling curled into my chest as he inhaled the meth, then carefully placed the pipe on the coffee table. Next, he handed me a beer. I cautiously grabbed the bottle and tried not to wince when I downed a sip. "It's all right." I chuckled without a trace of humor.

"You'll get used to it." Dad clamped his heavy palm on my back, then busied himself with the pipe again. "Not this stuff, though, Brayden. Just the alcohol. Stick to drinking, kid."

As my father instructed, I didn't touch the drugs. I didn't like what meth did to him. It turned him into a frantic and paranoid person. He considered everything and everyone to be his enemy. He accused family and friends of stealing from him. Dad thought everyone was out to get him.

One night he thrust a loaded shotgun in my hand, pushed me behind the stove and made me his watchdog. Positioned on my knees, I saw Dad crouched in front of me, clutching a pistol directed at the tiled kitchen floor.

"You see this?" Dad messily swiped his hand across his nose as sweat glided down his reddened face. He roughly situated the butt of the gun against my shoulder. "Keep the gun pulled into your shoulder, with your left hand holding onto the hand stock. You got that?"

"Ye-yeah," I stuttered. My voice trembled, and my breathing became more ragged by the second as Dad squeezed me behind the stove. "I just ... why am I doing this? Why do I —"

"Why the hell do you think you're doing this, boy?" Dad pointed a finger in my face and narrowed his brows. "There are folks after me — people who'll hurt you and your sisters just to get to me. You can't be in this business and not make enemies."

"Okay. Okay, I got it, Dad." I nodded, but I still deemed him nuts. He was too hyped up on drugs, and it was messing with his thinking. I just wanted to get my sisters away from him and run. *Run where?* I didn't even know. I just wanted to leave his home and find another.

"If anyone, *and I mean anyone*, comes through that front door," Dad jerked his head toward the front door, the same door I had the heavy shotgun aimed at, "you shoot them if you don't know them. You shoot them down, Brayden. Don't hesitate."

"Okay," I barely whispered. "Okay, I got it." I didn't know what else to say.

Dad leapt to his feet and paced the kitchen floor. He murmured to himself, his voice low and rough. His bloodshot eyes bulged as he ran his hands through his hair. My knees shook as I tried to keep my eyes and the shotgun pointed at the door. I kept peeking up at Dad. His erratic movements made me more on edge. I flinched when he suddenly squatted down to face me again, his nose inches from my own.

"You'd better take this, too." He slid the pistol to me.

Again, Dad hopped to his feet and turned on his heels. He strutted throughout our home, on a mission to guard his kids from supposed danger. Tired of kneeling, I dropped to my bottom and folded my legs. Even when my bawling began, I kept the gun trained on the door. I muttered prayers in the coldness of the night — something I hadn't done in years.

"God, please," I gasped and hiccupped between my cries. "Please don't let anyone come in that door. I don't want anyone to hurt my sisters, but I don't want to shoot anyone, either."

After that incident, Dad turned on me. He accused me of sleeping with his girlfriend. Seemingly overnight, he'd put me in the same category as everyone else he believed to be his enemy. He told me to leave his house, so I did.

My sisters and I moved in with my mother and her new husband. I hadn't had many dealings with him, but I expected he'd be just like the other men in her life. They claimed they would love her, treat her right and take care of her. They always turned out to be liars, though.

Randy was no different.

He brutally beat Mom and said cruel things to my sisters and me. He had a way of making Mom feel so horrible about herself, and I couldn't stand being around him. Just watching him treat Mom like that disgusted me. I wasn't strong enough to keep him away from Violet, Ella, Mom and myself. I was no good to them. And that angered me even more.

I didn't want to be like my father — too strung out on meth and plugged up on alcohol to function properly. I didn't want to be like Randy and my mother's other men — chasing women, beating women and feeding them lies. And I definitely didn't want to be like Julius — so twisted that he resorted to molesting young boys. All the men I'd ever encountered were beyond horrible. If that's what it took to be a man, then I didn't want to grow up to be one.

I figured I needed to die.

I burst out the front door, Mom and Randy still in the house fighting and bickering over nonsense. I tramped down the driveway and toward the dense woods. I spared a glance back. The sun hid behind Mom's little yellow house, painting a fiery burning color through the sky and casting shadows into the woods. Night would fall in just a few minutes, and I couldn't think of a better time to end my life — in complete darkness.

Nobody will miss me. Why would they? The way my life is, nobody cares.

The words taunted me as I pushed the gun into my scalp. Hot tears slipped down my cheeks and neck. I pressed my head against a tree, my finger hugging the trigger.

They'll never care, I told myself. *You can't be like them, Brayden. You can't keep living. This is the only way out. Just end the cycle, or else you're bound to be like them.*

I pulled the trigger.

No bang. No flash. No darkness.

Nothing.

I wept harder as I dragged the gun from my head and it suddenly fired on its own. I tossed it to the ground and dropped to my knees as my cries overcame me. I buried my head in my palms, my shoulders hunched over, racked with sobs. I tried to scramble to my feet, but I was so weak and so afraid of what I'd almost done that I could only sit there, crying out. I didn't know who I was crying to. I just cried, begging for some kind of help.

And that's when I heard a soft voice, like a whisper in my ear.

They need you.

I turned around but saw no one. I clambered to my feet and peered deeper into the woods, searching at every angle. No one was there. After a few minutes, I guessed the voice had to have come from inside me — my conscience telling me that I couldn't leave my sisters and mother behind.

They needed me.

In that moment, I decided to fight back. I'd fight anyone who tried to harm my mother or Violet and Ella. I'd fight any man who tried to ever take advantage of me again. I'd fight back against any sort of calamity that tried to ruin me. I wasn't going out by my own hand. I grabbed my pistol, tucked it in my waistband and walked home. The whole way, I told myself that the voice I'd heard definitely came from my conscience. There was no other explanation.

But deep down, *really deep*, I knew it had to be more than that.

❧❧❧

After I tried to kill myself, blind rage set in. I moved from place to place, never finding a suitable home. I couldn't live with my father because of his drugs and paranoia. I couldn't stay with Mom because I fought her husbands all the time — they all came with the same old bull, so I offered them a beating to let them know Mom had a son looking out for her. Each time she remarried, I knew the new jerk would be just like the last jerk.

After a while, I ended up living in a truck camper until my aunt Rhoda found out and invited me into her home. I attended college for a year and got serious with a girl I thought I'd start my life with. When she cheated on me, I decided to start fresh. I wanted a new campus, new people, a new town.

I joined the Marines at 19 years old. I'd grown so accustomed to fighting my mother's husbands, looking after my sisters, trying to take care of my mom and watch out for my dad, too. I desired to find myself and discover what I wanted to do with my life.

While away, my grandparents, aunts and uncles, parents and a few older ladies from my grandmother's church wrote to me. They talked about God in their letters — like they were on a mission to get me connected with God or just raise my awareness of him. Sometimes I'd lie in my bunk and read their letters and wonder if I should start praying or not.

Will it change my life? Will God want to hear from me? Will he even answer?

"Son, I'm so proud of you, and I respect what you're doing." My mother's letter choked me up as I cherished each word. "I respect what you're doing, Brayden. You're not doing what your parents have done. You're choosing a better way for yourself. A life. And just know that I'm praying for you all the time. I'm praying that God takes care of you and that you come back to me. I love you."

Mom is praying for me? That amazed me. *She's proud of me? She respects me?*

"I miss you, Brayden," my grandmother's letter read. "I pray for you every day. We all pray for you. While you're gone, I hope you really think about God. Think about giving your life to Jesus. You've been through so much. You've been through things no one even knows about, I'm sure. I know your life hasn't been easy. Just know that God has always been there. He's still with you. All you have to do is turn to him. God can pull you through anything. He loves you."

Many of the letters expressed similar thoughts. My aunts and uncles wrote about how much they missed me and hoped I returned safely. The love and support they poured out astounded me. I'd never realized how loved I was until I left home.

All my life, I'd concentrated on all the bad parts. How could I not, though? The addictions my parents battled on a daily basis affected me and my sisters so drastically. The throbbing ache and fury I felt as a result of their mistakes was steadily ruining me. Julius' actions branded me deep within. I didn't know how to get over what he'd done. I didn't think I ever would.

I began taking time to recognize how loving and caring my grandparents had always been to my sisters and me. I thought of Aunt Rhoda and how she allowed me to stay with her in order to finish high school. I remembered the times Mom told me she loved me. Even if Mom couldn't love herself, I always knew she loved me.

Through those letters, God showed me that even when I believed I was unloved and cast aside, I'd always been someone to him. I'd always been someone to many members of my family, although I sure hadn't felt like it. I learned there had always been people who tried to love me. Even Shyanne's family tried to love my sisters and me. What Julius did — I didn't blame Shyanne and her parents. That was on him. They didn't know he hurt me like that.

The letters encouraged me. They prompted me to pray and pay attention to God. I felt myself growing closer to him — like I wasn't alone anymore. All my life I'd felt alone, moving from house to house without ever having a real home. I realized God had always been with me, no matter where I was. I decided God would be my home.

During a 12-mile climb with my squad, I heard the same voice I'd heard after my failed suicide attempt. It was louder this time. As my hand gripped the solid rock of a mountain, the words whispered in my ear, just as they did when my gun misfired.

They need you.

For that short moment, I ignored the calls from the guys on my squad. I glanced down at the greenery beneath me, then gazed up at the cloudless sky. My eyes squinted from the brightness, as I tried to make sense of the words.

I had no business hearing those words at that moment. I wasn't trying to kill myself, depression wasn't an overwhelming feeling for me anymore and I had no intentions of leaving my family by dying anytime soon.

"God?" I warily whispered. My heart beat rapidly against my chest. "Who needs me?"

When I climbed down from that mountain with the other Marines, I made my mind up to give my life to God. I wanted to follow the teachings of Jesus and live the way my grandparents lived. I wanted to know how it felt to give my life to God. I didn't really seek anything in return from him at that moment, I just knew my heart wanted him. Still, I had a feeling God could take my pain away. I had a feeling he could help me forgive the people who'd harmed me.

I suspected he could change *everything.*

గం గం గం

When I returned home, I fell in love with a girl named Nedra, and we got married. I was 25 years old. Over the years, I'd grown so close to God. I read my Bible daily, my prayers to him seemed so personal and familiar, and I attended a church where several of my family members belonged. I secured a good job, and I thought life was actually looking up.

A couple years later, I believed God called me to become a preacher — someone to deliver uplifting and truthful messages about the awesomeness of God to people all over. I wanted to spread God's love, the greatness of Jesus Christ and tell people about how God can change their life. When I began preaching, my life took a turn I could have never predicted.

Nedra couldn't stay faithful to me. She cheated on me four times, and I forgave her each time. Her infidelity kept happening, though, and I couldn't keep allowing her to mistreat me or taint our marriage. She soon left me for another man, and I turned my back on God.

After the divorce, I fell apart. Old feelings returned — of being unloved, not good enough and less of a man. I lost my desire to preach and took up bad habits I hadn't touched for years. I went to clubs and bars to drown my misery with shots and beers. Alcohol became my crutch and a place to hide from the pain I felt. I slept around, arrived at work with banging hangovers and tried to hide my wild living.

All the while, I kept "playing church." I went to church services, sang the songs of love and devotion to God with the members there and acted like the same old Brayden. I thought I had everyone around me fooled, but I only fooled myself. It wasn't until the church leaders asked me to teach a class for the youth that I really took a look in the mirror.

"Brayden." Uncle Clyde cornered me at work one day and eyed me with a raised brow. "I heard about the church asking you to teach that class to the youngsters. You know you can't teach a class doing what you're doing."

"Doing what I'm doing?" I scoffed and leaned against the wall, checking my wristwatch. "What are you talking about, man?"

"What am I talking about?" He laughed humorlessly. "I'm talking about all the girls you're sneaking around with, son. I'm talking about the partying and drinking. How can you teach others, especially teenagers, about Christ when you're not even following his teachings? You've got to clean yourself up before you take on something like that. You know that."

"Look." I sighed and rubbed my eyes. "Just calm down. I told them I'd think about it."

"No, Brayden. Every day you walk in here smelling like alcohol or last night's conquest. I'm not dumb." He squeezed my shoulder and lightly shook me. "I know Nedra ripped a hole in your heart, but if you're not willing to completely change your ways and live for God, then you have no business telling others to do the same. I'm just speaking the truth. And if you didn't know this already, you would have never stopped preaching. You know right from wrong, kid."

I nodded, unable to argue with him. I'd fallen so far from God and felt so ashamed for turning my back on him. It didn't matter if I still attended church services and went through the motions of being a good Christian. I had to live the way Jesus required me to live, even when folks weren't looking.

I couldn't drink and sleep my misery away. I couldn't mask my sorrow in beer and women. The only way to cure my pain from the divorce was to give it over to God. Though no one knew it, I'd never truly given God my other old wounds to fix. Like what happened with Julius. I'd simply tucked it away and tried to forget it.

However, I found myself in way over my head. I knew the emotions that rose in my heart when Jesus entered my life. I knew how it felt to receive God's forgiveness and be given a chance to live a better life. And to know that I'd left those feelings behind because of the hurt from my divorce? I disappointed myself.

I depended on the temporary pleasure from sex and alcohol to ease my hurt instead of trusting God to mend my broken pieces together again. *Lord, how could I have left you? You're the one who's always been there. Only you offer permanent joy. How did I forget that?*

"God, what am I doing?" I knelt beside my bed. "You've brought me a long way … and here I am, turning away from you and living a way I know you don't approve of. Forgive me, God."

That's when I heard it again. The voice. The voice that spoke the same three words.

They need you.

It was stronger this time and clearer. Suddenly, I understood the words.

Of course they need me, I thought. *The youngsters I can relate to. The ones who have been through hell and back again. The ones misused, abused, forgotten, unloved and uncared for. They need me to tell them they're not alone in their hurt and there is hope.*

Hope in Christ.

I rededicated my life to the Lord that night. I apologized for going off his course for my life and tried my hardest to renew and strengthen my relationship with God. I let go of the alcohol and gave up sex — I leaned on God to support me, because I knew self-restraint would be tough to maintain at first. However, God helped me. I read my Bible more and took on the assignment of teaching the teenagers at my church about living for God.

As I continued to cling onto Jesus tighter than I had before, I started asking God to send me a wife. I wanted a wife that he wholeheartedly approved of and knew would love me for me. Part of me had always believed I wasn't good enough for Nedra because of the molestation in my past. That somehow *he* tainted me. I asked God to send me someone who would accept me, even for the crap that happened in my childhood.

That's when I met Kelly. She came to church with her son one Sunday, and it didn't take long for me to be drawn to her. She laughed at my little jokes. Her little son made me smile, and I could see myself being part of his life. Kelly spoke with such wisdom and kindness. She intrigued me.

I asked her to lunch, and as we sat across from one another at a restaurant, I laid my thoughts out on the table.

"Before we get really attached to one another, we need to talk about a few things. Is that all right with you?"

Kelly nodded. "Of course. Go ahead."

"As you know, I go to church." I rubbed at my chin and softly smiled. "God is first in my life, and if we're going to be together, I want God to be first in our relationship. I need him to be our foundation, Kelly. I've been in past relationships in which I didn't put God first, and they failed. I can't have that happening again. I refuse to put God on the back burner."

Kelly bit her lip, as if to stop from grinning. "Okay. Keep going."

"Right." I cleared my throat. "I don't mean to offend you, or even scare you, when I say this, but we will not have any physical contact until we're married. I'm not starting this relationship off wrong. We are not having sex.

I won't be staying the night at your house, and you won't stay the night at mine. I, uh, I want to stay firm with that, Kelly."

"Wow." Kelly's eyes brightened as she smiled. "Brayden, I can't believe you said that. I feel the same way. I know abstinence is hard, but when you have someone completely dedicated to the same, it's just, wow." She threw her hands up and laughed.

The following year, Kelly and I got married. Her son Isaac became my son, and I loved her even more for allowing me to be a father to him. We experienced some typical marital squabbles, but because we loved Jesus, we always worked out our problems with a strong belief that God would keep our marriage intact. As the years passed, we had more children. Amelia and Josiah became part of our little family, and we built a home for ourselves.

A real home.

꙳꙳꙳

In my early 30s, I attended an event called Men's Encounter, a function designed to bring Christian men together to bond, encourage one another and grow closer to God. There, I learned something about myself. I always knew that what happened with Julius damaged me, and it was something I never truly got over. During the event, I learned it was time to let it go.

"I have a secret I need to tell you," I said to Kelly one day. I felt her tense beside me and ease away from me, but

I quickly tugged her back. "It's just something that I know I need to tell you, I'm just not ready yet." I watched her swallow and nod her head with a timid smile. I sighed, relieved that I'd at least gotten that much out.

While I still struggled with telling Kelly about what happened in my childhood, we made the decision to look for a new church to attend. As we'd grown older and entered new areas of our life together, we believed God was leading us on a new path. A friend invited me to attend LifePoint Church, and my family enjoyed the service. The music and the inspirational Jesus-centered message really captivated us.

God, I need you to show me if this is where we're supposed to go, I thought as we drove away from LifePoint. *Is this the church you want me to bring my family to?*

"Hey, Dad," Isaac piped up from the backseat. "Are we going back to that church?"

"Yeah, Daddy!" Amelia kicked her small feet in excitement. "Are we going back?"

I glanced at Kelly and grinned at the lopsided smile on her face as she awaited my answer. "Well." I faltered. "What do you guys think? Should we go back or no?"

"Yeah!" Amelia giggled. "I want to go back to the surely alive church."

I laughed and peeked at her in the rearview mirror. "Surely alive?"

"You know. My God's not dead, he's surely alive! Like the song says."

As the kids started singing the song together, Josiah babbling along with them, I took that as my answer that God wanted us to be at LifePoint Church. Just months later, we became members, and all the love that the members bestowed upon our family inspired me to finally tell Kelly about my past. She took my confession well. She didn't judge me for what happened, and she didn't blame me. I always knew she loved me, but after I cried to her about what happened and she simply held me close and spoke kind words to me, I really knew she loved *all of me*.

Three weeks after I told Kelly about the abuse, I told my story to teenage guys at church I helped mentor. I then told the men's group at LifePoint. I stood before so many faces I hadn't known for very long, and I believed God told me to trust them, assuring me that they loved me unconditionally and that they needed to hear my story.

"You always hear that one of the worst things that could ever happen to a young one is child molestation, to be taken advantage of and tainted at such a young age." Tears streamed down my face, but I didn't care about crying in front of all those men. I believed guys in that audience needed to hear my story, because everyone suffers hurt in some way. "And it's true. It's a horrible thing for anyone to endure. It's gnawed at me for decades. It's hurt me from the very first time it happened. But I thank God that I can stand here today and say God healed me from that pain. He's helped me forgive what that guy did to me."

After I finished my speech, everyone clapped and

commended me for having the guts to tell such a dark secret. I made sure they knew that any strength I had came straight from God. One guy even approached me to talk about his own past.

"What you just did up there, Brayden," the young man began while shuffling his feet. "I, uh. I never could have told so many people that. It happened to me, too." He paused and roughly wiped at his eyes. "You opened my eyes. I thought I was the only one this ever happened to."

After I talked to him, other guys approached me with the same news. Some asked me to pray with them, and some just wanted to talk. That day, God showed me just how exhilarating it felt to be completely free in Christ Jesus. My past couldn't keep me down any longer.

꙲꙲꙲

Letting Jesus enter my heart was the best decision of my life. He gave me peace. He gave me a loving family and home. He erased the rage, hate and hurt that followed me from my past. He gave me the love to forgive all the people who ever wronged me and even urged me to pray for them. I once feared church and God, but I came to love church and am constantly chasing after God's heart. Just like God changed me and my life, I believe he can change anyone and any situation.

I started to mentor guys who've endured all kinds of things. I help them find the freedom that comes from giving their pain to Jesus. I always tell them, "Ask God to help you forgive the people who hurt you, for hurt people tend to hurt other people." With the help of God, I'm teaching the young men that just because their life started off a certain way, doesn't mean it has to end the same. They don't have to be a product of their environment or worst experiences. God speaks to us, even when our life is in a shambles. He's always there, knocking on the doors of our heart, asking to enter.

It's up to us to let him in.

FAILING INTO LOVE
THE STORY OF TIM AND TINA
WRITTEN BY ARLENE SHOWALTER

Tim

Should I do this? I paused, my finger poised over the "enter" button on my laptop.

Maybe not.

I ran a hand through my hair and thought of my son Ian sleeping in the next room. *I don't want to do anything that could hurt him.*

I stood up and went to the kitchen for a cup of coffee. As I passed Ian's room, I paused and opened the door. The hall light illuminated my sleeping 2-year-old, clutching his favorite teddy bear. I smiled, then frowned. "I never wanted to put you through a divorce, buddy. Never expected to be a single father. I can't risk your happiness for another woman."

Resolved, I returned to my computer. "Nope. Won't risk it."

I sat down and stared around the empty room.

"But, I'm so lonely." I groaned. "How can I stand it?"

જ જ જ

My dad checked out of my life before my younger brother was born. After that, our family consisted of Mom, Grandma, me and Jonathan.

Even though a year and a half younger than me, Jonathan quickly passed me up in height and weight and carried himself like a miniature linebacker, while I remained puny. The perfect target for classmates and teachers.

"Swing your arms, like this," Miss Bloom, my kindergarten teacher, instructed. Pretty soon all my classmates looked like little windmills while I hugged my own arms close to my chest.

"Tim, move your arms! We are exercising together."

I stared at my sneakers and bit my trembling lips. Even at 5, I had already learned that no matter what I did or how I did it, the other kids laughed and teased me.

"Tim." Her voice raised a notch, and she frowned. "Move your arms *right now*, or you'll be in trouble."

I squeezed my eyes shut to keep the tears in check. I heard her feet snapping across the floor, and suddenly she jerked my arms up.

"Move your arms!"

I plopped my butt on the ground and wished myself somewhere else. The other kids snickered and snorted.

More than once, teachers singled me out only for my fellow students to follow their example. Boys punched me, and girls pinched me. If I yelled at them, teachers typically came to the bullies' defense. I hated them all.

As Jonathan got older and joined me at school, he would come to my defense during every playground confrontation — his fists flying and mouth grinning, always ready to stand in for his short, nerdy brother. We grew close and stayed that way.

ॐॐॐ

"I have to take Jonathan to the doctor today," Mom told me when he was 14. "He wants to run tests to see why he's losing weight and can't shake this flu."

"Where's Jonathan?" I asked Mom a few days later when I got home from school.

"When we went to the doctor's for the results of the tests, he said he wanted him admitted to the hospital."

"For the *flu*?"

"It's leukemia," Mom told me.

"Leukemia? What does that mean?"

"It means his body isn't producing white blood cells to fight infection. That's why he keeps getting sick."

"Oh. Can we go see him tonight?"

"Of course, but don't tire him out."

Tire out Jonathan? He's tough. Whatever leukemia is, it can't keep him down. He's gonna lick this thing.

Jonathan got better and then got sick again. Every time he went into the hospital, I'd hang out in his room. We played video games together and enjoyed the same closeness we had on the "outside."

Then the doctors transferred Jonathan to St. Jude's in Memphis, Tennessee.

Grandma and I stayed home, while Mom traveled to

the hospital. After several hospitalizations there, the cancer went into remission and life resumed as before.

෪෪෪

"I'm going to join the Army when I graduate," I told my family.

"Why?" Mom asked. "What about college?"

Are you kidding? Every memory I have of school stinks.

"I'm done with school."

I finished Basic Training in South Carolina and moved on to Ft. Gordon, Georgia, for Advanced Individual Training, or AIT. I called home a lot to keep up on Jonathan's progress.

"Hey, Tim, your mom's on the phone."

"Oh, no." Dread squeezed my heart like a boa. *She usually waits for my calls.* My government-issue boots seemed extra heavy as I trekked to the communal phone.

"Jonathan's back in St. Jude's." Her voice sounded tired.

"Don't worry, Mom. I'll go visit him this weekend when I get leave."

Some Army buddies and I drove over. We joked and swaggered on our way to his room. Suddenly, reality smacked me upside the head. Jonathan lay like a pale, almost-hairless gnome with machines clicking and whirling and clacking all around him. *He'll be all right,* I tried to convince myself. *He's always pulled through before.*

I returned to base but continued calling Mom frequently, always asking about my brother. A few months later, she told me, "You need to come home."

"Is it that serious?"

"Yes. I brought Jonathan home. He's on hospice care now. If you want to say goodbye, you need to get here as fast as you can."

"Hey, Jonathan." I sat next to my brother's bed.

He dragged his eyes open.

"You'll be okay, buddy. Just hang in there."

A slight nod.

I pinched my eyes shut. A feeling of failure hit me hard. *He's my brother. Why can't I fix this for him? Why?*

Jonathan slipped out of our lives a few hours later.

I endured the funeral in stony silence. *Don't tell me about a loving God. Where was he when Jonathan got sick? Why didn't he heal him? He could if he were really God like all these people keep babbling.*

Introverted before, I became even more withdrawn. The Army sent me to Germany, where I soon acquired a taste for the local beer. Alcohol helped fuzz out memories of bullies. Growing up without my father. My dead brother.

In some ways, the Army forced me to interact with people. Trusting your fellow soldier could mean the difference between life and death. But, once alone in my room, I locked the door and unlocked the tears.

I finished my enlistment in New Mexico, continued drinking and partying and started having one-night flings. After the Army, I found a job that forced me to work long hours and travel frequently. I welcomed any distraction from heavy thinking, while hoping I could drink myself numb.

❧❧❧

After three years, I suffered burnout and returned home to Lebanon, Missouri, to be close to Mom again. I moved in with a couple of Jonathan's friends. Their acceptance of me helped turn me away from alcohol and stop sleeping around. We often spent our weekends following local bands.

One day, as I visited a skateboard shop, a cute girl noticed the cap I wore, emblazoned with the name of a favorite band.

"I like their music, too," Kim said.

We began discussing their music and other bands we admired and soon found out we shared similar taste in music.

Although I remained very quiet, shy and awkward, Kim's outgoing nature thawed me enough for me to fall in love. We married, and she quickly got pregnant.

The romance bled out of our marriage faster than a one-hit wonder. Kim endured a difficult pregnancy and most attempts at conversation ended in fights. *Everything will be okay after our baby is born,* I told myself countless times.

I gazed down at our sleeping newborn, amazed and dazed. *We made that! He's a part of me and a part of Kim.*

The marriage soured further. Kim looked for reasons to fight, while I searched for peace.

"I want out of this marriage," she complained, well before our second anniversary.

"I can't do that. I grew up without a father. I can't do that to our son."

I slugged through a marriage that Kim refused to invest in, desperate to save my son from repeating my own history. *I can't let him grow up without a father.*

Kim followed me around the house, nagging and complaining. Misery dogged my days and haunted my nights. I often escaped upstairs to play computer games in solitude.

"You're chatting with women!" Kim had snuck up behind me. I jumped.

"No, I'm not. I'm playing this game with another dude."

"Liar."

"Here." I shoved the keyboard at her. "Want to chat with him and find out?"

"What *I want* is out. As in, *out* of this marriage."

"We'll make it work."

"I don't want to make it work. And, for your

information, I've been sleeping with your friend Chuck. What do you think of that?"

My heart crumpled as she packed a few things and slammed out the door, taking our son with her.

I've failed again. I collapsed on the sofa and buried my head in my hands. "Why couldn't I find a way to keep her happy?" I muttered to myself. "Why couldn't I fix our marriage? I'm done with the relationship scene. I'm going to concentrate on Ian and be the best father a boy ever had, even if Kim and I aren't together any longer."

Kim started leaving Ian with me more and more until I was almost his full-time caregiver. I reveled in the opportunity to raise my son but continued to miss female companionship — struggling to meet all Ian's needs while resisting my own.

One night when Ian was still 2, I began surfing through profiles on MySpace. One particular lady caught my eye. In every picture she posted, her smile seemed as wide as the Missouri River. That appealed to me after enduring Kim's scowls and complaints.

Do I really want to do this?

I typed out a greeting, then erased it. I paced my living room, got a cup of coffee, looked in on Ian and returned to the computer. *Do I really want to do this?*

Tina

I looked at the message on my MySpace page. *I see you support the local music scene. I know Zach, too. He* mentioned a drummer I'd posted a picture of on my page. I knew him from following his band. He wrote a few more awkward words and signed off. *Tim.*

That's one weird dude, I thought, shaking my head. "Look, buster. I don't know enough about you to reply," I muttered to myself as I read his message. But I visited his page and saw we had several mutual friends.

"What do you think of Tim?" I asked my friends. "He's contacted me on MySpace, and I'm not interested in another sucky relationship."

"You'd like him," each answered. "He's really a nice guy. Funny. Give him a chance."

"Maybe. I've had enough bad relationships for one lifetime."

I sent back a cautious reply. Soon, I realized he was as careful as I. We seemed to circle the ring like reluctant boxers, each of us putting out a tentative jab but never a punch. I learned he had a son and seemed very protective of him. *I like that. Sounds like a good family man. Rare these days.*

We tiptoed into real phone conversations and soon learned we shared the same weird tastes. We both loved horrible B-rated horror movies from the 1980s.

"Have you ever seen *Phantom*?" Tim asked.

"Not yet."

"No? I can't believe it! It's super funny." He paused. "Say, how would you like to come over to my house and watch some movies on Saturday? Come around 9 p.m., after Ian's in bed."

"I guess I could." *I notice he invited me when his son would be sleeping.*

I realized he was protecting his son while I was fighting to protect my heart. By that time, I really wanted to meet him and battled my growing feelings for him.

Even though I was 24 and Tim 30, we acted like two awkward teens on our first date. We sat on the couch together, each stiff and trying to maintain personal space. Emotions raged inside me. *I like him even better in person.*

"Some of these movies are horrible," I said, well into our stay-in-and-watch-really-bad-horror-movies date.

"Yeah, but they get better every time you watch them."

"You've watched these more than once?"

"Yeah!"

Yep, he's weird.

"You doing anything special for Valentine's Day tomorrow?" Tim asked, interrupting my thoughts while he draped one arm casually around my shoulders.

"I'm going to a concert with some of my friends."

"I can totally go with you if you want. My ex is coming for Ian in the morning."

I smiled as I recalled the self-invite on the drive home. *He's definitely worth seeing again. Nerdy, but sweet.*

My friends had booked a hotel suite, where we stayed after the concert. One by one they drifted off to bed, leaving Tim and me talking on the couch.

FAILING INTO LOVE

৵৵৵

I knew he took his responsibility as a father seriously, wanting to guard against his son becoming attached to any woman who might take off as Kim had. And I struggled against falling for another manipulating and disingenuous male, so I decided I needed to settle my own heart, feelings and fears for good.

"I'm in the process of divorce," I said.

"So am I," Tim responded.

"My trust level of the male animal has waned to non-existent."

"I'm pretty much there with women," he agreed.

"I got into the party scene and drank hard when I was a pre-teen."

"I did the same in my early 20s. I drank to dull the pain of my brother's death." He went on to explain how important Jonathan had been to him, not only as a brother, but as a true friend. "It was so hard. The drinking did nothing to ease the pain, so I finally gave it up. Why did you take to booze?"

"My stepfather started molesting me when I was 8. Mom worked nights as a nurse. If I tried to avoid him, he beat up my little brother, so I sucked it up and took it. As soon as I discovered alcohol, I drank anything I could get my hands on and progressed to hard drugs."

"I'm sorry."

"It got worse. I realized he had no intention of quitting, so I decided to lose my virginity on my own terms. After he found out I had slept with a kid from school, he lost interest." I paused, waiting for the pain to ebb before continuing.

"After that, he beat my brother more. I could no longer protect him. Then, I got pregnant in high school and dropped out."

"I didn't know you have a kid."

"I don't. I gave it up for adoption at birth." *I'm going to throw every piece of crap that my life consists of at you, Tim-bo, and see how fast you run from me.*

He never flinched. We continued swapping stories of love and loss, pain and passion. Suddenly, Tim yawned and stretched.

"Good grief," he said, glancing at his watch. "Do you realize it's morning?"

"Already?" I laughed.

"Let's go get some breakfast."

"Sounds like a plan."

This guy's the real deal. I've never met a nurturing male in my whole life. They're all just takers and thieves. But, this guy really is different. I can see how much he loves Ian and is determined to protect him, even from me, if necessary.

ᕤᕤᕤ

Twelve weeks after crashing my concert-going group, Tim said, "Um, I know we're not kids, but, um, do you think you'd like to be my girlfriend?"

I laughed. "I'd love to."

We kept in constant contact — over the phone, through email and in person. Tim sent me goofy pictures of himself that he'd photo-shopped, and I fell even harder. I let down my guard about men, and he lowered the wall he kept around Ian.

"Want to move in with me?" he asked a few months later.

"Sure. I think that would be cool."

I called him later. "My grandmother is going through her things and wants us to come over and see if there's anything we can use."

Grandma rifled through several boxes in her garage. At last, she held up a cup. "I've got these cups," she said. "You can have them if you get married."

I looked over at Tim. He shrugged. "Are we planning a wedding?" he asked.

"Don't you *want* to plan one?" Grandma asked, raising one eyebrow and smiling.

A few days later, Tim and I took my grandparents to the mall. Grandma and Tim took off, while I trailed Grandpa.

An hour later, Grandma materialized, grinning, with Tim in tow. "Tim's bought you something," she said, "but if you don't like it, don't you lie about it. Just go ahead and tell him."

"You like it?" Tim asked, opening a tiny box and extending a beautiful ring toward me.

"Yes," I said.

"Good," he replied, reaching for my left hand. "Now, it's official."

We married a few months later, in a civil ceremony, in our yard.

჻჻჻

During the next two years, Ian and I bonded well while Tim and I looked forward to having more children and growing old together.

Then one day I awakened in severe pain.

"What's the matter, honey?" Tim bent over me, one hand gently stroking my forehead.

"I can't stand the pain," I gasped.

"What do you think it is?"

"I broke my back in an accident 10 years ago. Maybe that's what's causing it. I'm going to see a pain specialist. ASAP."

The pain worsened with each treatment. One night I lay in our bed, curled in a fetal position and sobbing.

"This is ridiculous," Tim said. "Pain specialist or no, I'm taking you to Emergency."

"You have a cyst on your ovary," the ER doctor informed me. "No big deal. Just get in to see your gynecologist as quickly as you can."

"You need surgery as soon as possible," Dr. Green told me after running tests. "You have five cysts. Some are as large as softballs. One is invading your sciatic nerve.

That's the cause of your extreme pain. We have to get in and remove them."

❧ ❧ ❧

I struggled to awaken after the surgery, the anesthesia clinging like unwanted humidity in July. Gradually, I made out the faces of Tim, my mom and her husband and my grandparents. Sadness covered each face.

"What's wrong?"

Tim rubbed his hands together. Mom glanced away. Grandma blinked back tears.

"Tell me what's going on," I demanded.

Tim stepped up and laid a hand on my own. "Honey, the doctor says we can't have kids. I'm so sorry."

"Wha — why?" I struggled to sit up.

"The doctor will be in soon." Mom moved closer. "It's rather technical. She can explain it all to you."

"The cysts killed your ovaries and ate up one fallopian tube," Dr. Green explained when she arrived that evening. "I had to remove one ovary and both tubes. I'm sorry."

I turned the disappointment into obsessive determination to solve my problem. Soon I focused on in vitro fertilization (IVF) and spent every possible minute educating myself. Armed with my hard-gained knowledge, I convinced Tim that we were ready to see a fertility expert. He laid out all the costs at our first appointment.

I struggled to justify the high cost with the low chance

of success — $10,000 to $15,000 for a 20 to 35 percent success rate. I withdrew, full of pain, regret and remorse. *Why did I give that baby up for adoption?* I calculated her age.

Maybe it's my fault for all the drugs I took and the heavy drinking. My world revolved around my childless state, and I lost all interest in intimacy.

Tim

Tina and I both sank into depression after the surgery, but for different reasons. I shared her disappointment that we couldn't have any more children, but more than that, I felt like a failure again. I couldn't fix Tina any more than I could fix my brother.

As a boy, I loved to take things apart and put them back together, always fascinated in learning how things worked. I got to where I could fix almost anything I put my hands and mind to, but I couldn't fix *people*. My brother. My first marriage. And, now, Tina.

We rotated in separate orbits, under the same roof, but separate nonetheless. We existed on autopilot, attending to our jobs, home chores and taking care of Ian when he came. We watched TV together, sat together on one couch, but a chasm of sorrow separated our thoughts and hearts.

The same loneliness returned that had gnawed at me when Kim left.

What could it hurt? I returned to MySpace, clicked on

the singles postings and soon found myself looking at online porn sites. *After all, I'm sure not getting any under my own roof. I don't deserve Tina's apathy. So what's the harm of indulging in a little virtual sex?*

Six months passed. One night, as I drove home from work, I stopped at a traffic light. My secret life had been bothering me, and every excuse I used to rationalize my behavior turned hollow. Suddenly, I *heard* a voice inside my head.

Tim, you'd better stop it.

"What?" I looked around at the other drivers. Nobody looked back. I checked the radio dial. Off.

Tim, you need to quit doing what you're doing right now.

I gripped the steering wheel and navigated a left turn. I wondered if God was actually speaking to me. The God I'd dumped when Jonathan died.

I had accepted Jesus as my Savior in my teens. Mom was ecstatic to see her son "saved." Mom's faith never wavered, even when divorce robbed her of a husband and death, a son.

At Jonathan's funeral, I heard all the usual religious prattle about God's goodness and leaning on him, blah, blah, blah. I couldn't accept that God any longer. *He* stole my brother from me.

But in that moment, I knew this same God was in the truck with me, warning me. Not because he was a mean God and wanted to see people suffer. But rather, because of his love. What mother, seeing her toddler walking to the end of a pier, would shrug? What father doesn't jerk his child back when the kid steps in front of traffic?

I *knew* I was stepping in front of a train, putting myself in the path of destruction. Suddenly, I realized how much I was betraying not just Tina, but also my son.

"Oh, God," I cried in the silence of the truck's cab. "How could I do this to the two people who mean the whole world to me? I could lose everything and for what?"

For what? God seemed to echo my question.

I pondered the sudden revelation as another mile rolled under my tires. Another red light stopped more than my vehicle as my thoughts tumbled forward.

"I've cheated myself, too, by lowering myself to such a base level. And you, God. I've dishonored you as well."

Unfamiliar tears pushed themselves free.

"God, I promise you I'm going to make it right, today, as soon as Tina comes home."

Tina

"I need to talk to you." Tim sat on our couch with an uncharacteristically somber expression. "Please sit down."

Oh, gosh, what did I do? My mind scrambled to think of something — anything — that could explain his sober face.

I sat on the edge of a chair.

"I have greatly wronged you," he began. "Not only you, but Ian. Myself. And God."

God? We didn't do "God" in our home.

"I've been watching porn and Internet sex for the past six months."

I felt like Tim slugged me in the stomach. My world bottomed out. Here, I'd finally found one man who was real, who never manipulated or used me. And he's saying he was willing to trash everything on porn? Internet sex? *You've got to be kidding me.*

I worked my jaw, but words froze in my mouth.

"I'm taking 100 percent responsibility," he continued. "This is by no means your fault. I screwed up big time, but …" He paused and searched my eyes.

"If you can find the strength to forgive me, I promise you I will get right with God. I knew him as a teen but got mad when Jonathan died. I've lived my life as I've pleased ever since. But, starting today, I'm putting God in the center of my life and our marriage. I'm going to go back to church and fly straight."

My head spun as I tried to wrap my mind around his confession *and* declaration. *This came out of nowhere. How could it happen? How can I trust that he's telling me the truth now?*

"Say something," he begged.

"It's not all your fault," I said. "We need to work on the level of communication we enjoyed when we dated."

"I agree."

"And, if you're serious, I want to renew our wedding vows. This time, I want you to hand-write yours to me."

"I will."

❧❧❧

I could work with those promises, but I wasn't too keen on the church thing. Mom's parents had been missionaries, and she rebelled. She encouraged her children to think like atheists.

When Tim dressed to go to church the following Sunday, Ian got excited.

"You coming, Tina?" He bounced up and down, clapping his small hands. *How can I turn him down?* Personally, I felt I was way too bad for God to love or forgive for the mess I'd made of my life before meeting Tim.

I watched my husband keep his promises — and more. At the pastor's invitation, he walked to the front of the worship space for prayer. I remained in my seat, wondering why folks needed to "go forward" to pray. *What good does it do, anyway?*

"All my life, I've loved to fix things," he explained on the way home. "Toys, broken radios. Anything I could get my hands on, I'd study and work at until I got it fixed. I got mad at God when I couldn't fix my brother, my marriage, our inability to conceive a child. Today, I realized I couldn't even fix myself. That's why I asked for prayer. I wanted to publicly acknowledge my total dependence on God for his help."

Tim changed overnight. Before, he groused and complained about anything and everything.

After, he worked hard to bring harmony and peace

into the home. He jumped in to help me with household chores.

I started warming up to this "God" he believed in. I relaxed at church. The singing moved me and softened my heart and attitude toward God and the people who believed in him.

I feel so comfortable here, I realized one day as the worship team began their third song. *This is the first time I've ever felt comfortable in my life!*

❧❧❧

Tim's friend Rex stepped into my place of work one day. "Tina, you and Tim should come over to LifePoint. I know you would really love it there. It's a great church."

"We'll see. We like where we are now."

I told Tim about Rex's visit over dinner.

"What do you think?" I asked.

"It might be nice to go," he said. "More opportunity to connect with others."

I still felt hesitant, so Ian and Tim went to LifePoint the next Sunday without me.

"You'd love it," Tim almost shouted when they returned home. "It's a great church."

"I like it!" Ian bounced on the balls of his feet. "I like it a lot."

I joined them the following Sunday. Within minutes, smiling people surrounded us.

"We're so happy to see you."

"So glad you came."

"Welcome to LifePoint!"

Okay, God, I prayed in my heart. *I'm ready to welcome you into my heart and serve you with all my being, just like Tim has.*

౿ ౿ ౿

After God helped us strengthen our marriage, Tim and I began looking into other avenues for having children besides IVF.

"Maybe adoption?" Tim suggested.

"I think I'm ready for that."

Not long after that, I got a phone call from a client. "Would you like to adopt a baby?"

Duh. "Of course!" I said. *That's a stupid question. I've only obsessed all over the place about it.*

"I know a girl who got pregnant and is planning to abort. Maybe I can convince her not to go through with it."

"Yes! Please! Let me know what she says."

"Hi, I'm Lily." The girl called me herself. "Do you want my baby?"

"Yes, Lily, I do."

"I'm glad." She sighed. "I'm a single mom already. I was raised to believe abortion is wrong. I just didn't know what else to do."

"Thank you, Lily. God bless you for this decision."

The months passed. I watched Lily's pregnancy progress with as much excitement as if I were pregnant myself. Tim and I accompanied her on all her doctor appointments and counted the days until we would hold our baby in our arms.

My best friend Darla threw a baby shower for me in late spring. The day before the event, I felt horribly sick at work.

"Wouldn't it be funny if you were pregnant," she said, laughing, "now that you're going to adopt?"

"Ha-ha. Not amused. Thanks for the sympathy while I'm puking all over the place here."

Still, I stopped at a drugstore on my way home and bought a pregnancy test.

"What's that for?" Tim asked.

"I threw up at work, and Darla joked about me being pregnant now that we're adopting. I'm going to take the test and then send her a picture of the results just to shut her up. Then the joke will be on her."

I went to the bathroom, peed on the stick and tossed it on the edge of the sink. A few minutes later, I remembered it as I dried my hands.

What? I bent closer. Positive. I grabbed the towel bar for support because I thought I'd pass out and screamed, "Tim, Tim!"

"What is it?" he asked, throwing open the bathroom door. "Are you hurt?"

I gestured at the test strip. He looked at it and grinned. *Almost like he already knew. Hmmm.*

"This is impossible," I gasped. "We need to get back to the store and buy one kit of every brand they have."

"With pleasure!"

We returned home with four more test kits. Every last one showed positive.

"Wait until Darla sees this," I said, reaching for my cell phone. I lined up all five strips, snapped a picture and sent it to her.

"You'd better not be messing with me," Darla texted back.

I told my surprise news at the shower the next day, and the party became a huge celebration.

"Two kids!"

"Isn't God good?"

"Just like him. To surprise you like that."

"Double blessings."

❧❧❧

In all the excitement, worry nagged at me. "I just can't rest until I know the baby is settled in the right place."

Eight weeks and three days after I first took the test, I readied for my first ultrasound.

"There she is," the technician pointed.

"It's real." I stared at the little glob on the screen and grabbed Tim's hand.

"Our very own little gummy bear."

❧❧❧

Excitement soared as we waited for the births of *two* children, but less than a month from her due date, Lily called.

"I'm sorry," she sobbed into the phone, "but I can't give this baby up. I've grown to love her. I just can't do it."

"It's okay, Lily. God bless you for keeping the child and not aborting. I know you will be happy."

I kept my voice light, but my heart broke for the baby I'd never hold as my own. Then I rubbed my own tummy. "God, you are so good. You gave us this child, this miracle child, just at the right time."

Dr. Green had told us that my one fallopian tube had re-grown. "It's nothing short of a miracle," she said.

I couldn't help but thank God because we were a small part in keeping Lily's baby alive. She didn't go through with the abortion when she found out we wanted to adopt, and we'd always be thankful for that.

☙☙☙

God brought as much life into my soul as he did my womb.

Tina, you need to forgive your stepfather. I sensed God speaking deep within my heart.

How can I? After all those years of molestation and abuse?

So his misdeeds were worse than your own? Didn't you use your boyfriend for sex just to get back?

I pondered that for some time. Sin is sin. How can I

rate my own wrongdoings lower than the wrongdoings of someone else, even my stepdad? And, what good had it done me to hang on to my anger toward him?

I've done nothing but hurt myself, I realized. *The past is the past, and nothing can change it, but how I chose to deal with it has colored every aspect of my life. It's done nothing but make me miserable. I'm going to release it all right now into your hands, God, and start focusing on all the positive things in my life.*

And you? I felt God probing further. *Are you ready to forgive yourself, also?*

Well ...

I've forgiven you.

I realized how silly it was not to forgive myself if God already had.

After that, I felt more freedom every day. LifePoint has helped me on this journey through people's genuine love, the amazing worship music and Pastor Kelly's concise and relevant messages.

Tim

My life turned around when I met the real God who loves me — flaws and all — and not the god I had conjured up in my embittered heart. I came to see God is the one true Mr. Fix-it. Not only did he fix my heart, my family and my life, he *healed* them all. So I learned to thank God for everything — even for all my failures, real and imagined. Those failures caused me to fall into *his* love.

TIME OF DEATH
THE STORY OF TORI
WRITTEN BY ELLEN R. HALE

My two young sons enjoyed the excitement of Christmas morning, thrilled with the presents Santa had brought to Missouri for them.

But my phone rang in the afternoon, and as soon as I saw the call was coming from a California hospital, I had only one thought.

What has their father done now?

"Is this Tori?" a woman asked.

"Yes."

"We need to talk to you about Alan."

"Is he drunk?"

I assumed my husband, an alcoholic, had too much to drink again. We had separated a few months earlier.

"He tried to kill himself," the nurse explained. "We resuscitated him on the scene, but now he's at the hospital on life support."

"What did he do? Did he drink too much?" I questioned the nurse, anger in my voice.

"When we tested his blood-alcohol level, it was extremely over the legal limit for intoxication. However, he hung himself."

Alan had left for California before Christmas. He was staying with friends who returned home to find Alan hanging in the garage. They pulled him down and called 911.

"We've done numerous tests, and he's only living because of the machines," the nurse continued. "He has no brain function."

I began to cry.

"You are still his wife, and you have the legal right to decide what happens to him."

The next morning, I raced to board a flight to California. After I arrived, I rented a car and drove to the hospital.

I stepped off the elevator and saw one of my aunts in a waiting room. Not a single one of Alan's family members or friends was there.

I spoke to the nurses before entering Alan's room. I could not believe what he looked like. He had always kept his head shaved and sported a mustache and goatee, but he'd grown some hair.

The machines beeped. I smelled death. My anger grew.

Where are his father, brother and sister? No wonder he killed himself. He had no one supporting him here.

Then Alan's dad called and asked me to wait for him before turning off the machines. So I sat down, remembering how Alan treated me worse and worse during our years together. Regardless of the pain I had endured, I still loved him. He was the father of my boys. He had called Christmas morning to talk to our 4-year-old son and found out I was spending the holiday with George, a co-worker of mine. I had started a relationship with George after leaving Alan that fall. I started to feel responsible for the suicide.

Once Alan's father appeared, I told the nurses to shut off the machines. He stopped breathing after a few minutes, and the heartbeats displayed on the monitor changed to a flat line. The hospital staff called the time of death. Alan's dad turned around and walked out of the room, saying nothing.

Later, he contacted me to ask that Alan be cremated and that he receive his remains. I agreed, not wanting to argue. I signed a paper for the nurses, and they handed me Alan's wallet.

I stayed in California for two days, unable to control my emotions. I couldn't handle his death, so I headed back to Missouri before his cremation. To make the situation worse, his family began blaming me for his death. *What if we had stayed together? What if I had sought more help for his alcoholism?* Alan had tried rehab programs and Alcoholics Anonymous, with little success.

The last call he made on his cell phone was to my number, so maybe Alan's family was right. *What had our son and I said to make him kill himself?*

❧❧❧

In the counselor's office, I used dolls to show what my father had done to my body. He was charged with sexually abusing my older brother and me. But he hired an expensive attorney and was not convicted.

However, a judge granted my mother full custody. She successfully submitted a petition to move to California, where some of her family lived — partly to prevent my dad from abusing us further and partly so we wouldn't be recognized in town as the kids whose father molested them. I was only 5 years old when we settled in California.

Unfortunately, the move didn't protect me from further sexual activity. I longed for someone to love me, and when I was 10, I started sneaking around with the son of my mom's friend and having sex with him. Richard was four years older than me. I wrote about how much I cared for Richard in a journal, and my mom confronted me when she read it. I denied everything, but Richard admitted we had a sexual relationship. Child Protective Services ordered me to undergo counseling.

The therapist asked me why I thought having sex was okay at my age. I wouldn't answer any questions. My mom forbade me from spending time with Richard.

A few years later, we managed to find a way to be together again in secret. When our parents found out, they insisted we openly be boyfriend and girlfriend.

I was a freshman in high school, and Richard was a freshman in college about an hour away. I thought I loved him. After school dismissed each Friday, I headed for Richard's apartment and stayed with him through Sunday.

But after I graduated from high school, I broke up with Richard. I didn't really have a good reason. We had talked about getting married, but I decided I wanted to start hanging out with a different group of friends.

Richard cried on the front porch of his aunt and uncle's house when I told him I was done being his girlfriend. I broke his heart, but I didn't care. I felt almost no emotion toward him and simply wanted to move on.

I only remember seeing my father one time after we moved to California. Every Thanksgiving, we returned to Missouri to visit family, including my paternal grandparents. My father, his new wife and their two daughters came to my grandparents' house once when I was there. I sat in the living room, holding my little half-sister on my lap. I began crying uncontrollably. I hated my father, and I couldn't believe another woman married him and had children with him. *What is he doing to these girls? Is he hurting them like he hurt me?*

ॐ ॐ ॐ

As soon as I finished my full-time job each day, I stopped at the home I shared with my mom to change my clothes and grab a bite to eat. I left in my Volkswagen Jetta for the bars, where I used my fake ID to order mixed drinks, like Sex on the Beach or Long Island iced tea. I quickly became popular, playing pool and singing karaoke.

I stayed until the bar closed, either going home with my cousin or with a guy I'd met. After sleeping a few hours, I woke up early and returned home to shower, eat breakfast and dress for work. This routine helped me forget the pain of my childhood.

UNBROKEN

I met Alan at the bar. He knew my cousin. Many nights, I drove Alan home and hauled him into his apartment because he was so drunk. One morning about two years after we met, Alan's brother called with the news that their mom had committed suicide by overdosing on pills. Since Alan was hung over, I drove him to his brother's place and dropped him off.

The next day, I called him, and he didn't answer. He didn't return my calls, either. Alan shut me and his friends out of his life. In his absence, his best friend Jeff and I started playing pool together. At first we were just friends, but soon we started sleeping together. I moved into Jeff's apartment. This made Alan mad, but eventually he began partying with us again.

Jeff and I bought a beautiful house across the street from the waterfront. We hosted parties there. We enjoyed a fairy tale wedding — I felt like Cinderella. A woman Jeff knew picked up my bridesmaids and me and drove us to the ceremony in a carriage pulled by a white horse. When we arrived at the ceremony site along the waterfront, my grandfather walked me down the aisle. Many family members traveled from Missouri to attend our wedding.

At the reception, I danced with my grandpa. I also danced with Alan, who was Jeff's best man. The photos of Alan and me showed clearly that he still had feelings for me.

The next morning, Jeff and I departed on a cruise to Mexico. We explored the sea by scuba diving, and I loved dressing up for the fancy dinners on the ship.

When we returned home from our honeymoon, the fun with Jeff ended. I faced reality.

"Are you busy?" Alan asked over the phone. "I didn't bring my lunch today. Can you bring me a sandwich?" And so, I started taking lunch to Alan. Then I started sitting with him while he ate. Then Alan started calling me when he knew Jeff was working, and we started hanging out together.

The more time I spent with Alan, the more I realized I loved him. I had married Jeff because Alan had pushed me away after his mother's death. I felt miserable. I added vodka to my orange juice before work in the morning and smoked pot on my lunch hour to try to make myself feel better.

About five months after the wedding, I filed for divorce and moved in with my mom. I invited Jeff to lunch to discuss the details of our divorce.

"I'm pregnant," I admitted.

"Who is the father?"

"Alan."

Jeff didn't say much, but I could tell he was fuming inside. Our lunch ended abruptly. I began living with Alan before finalizing the divorce.

❧❧❧

"Where were you?" My voice boomed when Alan came home from a night of drinking.

He yelled at me in response, storming upstairs to our

office. "Who was here while I wasn't home?" I was six months pregnant.

Alan threw my computer and other belongings over the balcony. I charged up the stairs to try to stop him from destroying any more of my possessions. He pushed me hard, and I tumbled down the stairs. Fortunately, he didn't seriously injure me or the baby. I was just sore afterward.

Another night, we started fighting, and he fled in his Suburban. I followed him in my car. He finally stopped along the road. I stopped, too, and walked up to his window to talk to him. Instead, Alan turned the vehicle and struck me, knocking me to the ground and causing me to hit my head. I checked in at the emergency room so the doctors could make sure our baby hadn't been harmed. The staff asked me what happened, but I refused to tell the truth.

"I fell and hit my head," I lied.

A different kind of pain struck when I was eight months pregnant. I lay curled up on the living room floor with stomach pains, and my friend who was with me advised me to go to the doctor.

The doctors diagnosed me with appendicitis and ordered me to have surgery. If the baby was not in danger, they explained, they would leave him in the womb. If not, they would remove both my appendix and my son.

A severe storm affected the electricity, causing the lights to turn off and on. Alan showed up at the hospital right before I headed into surgery. I could tell he was drunk.

TIME OF DEATH

When the anesthesia wore off and I woke up, I was alone in a hospital room. I felt scared until the doctors shared the good news that they performed the appendectomy without delivering the baby. They prescribed bed rest for the remainder of my pregnancy. I had to stop working at my job and stay home.

Disregarding the doctors' orders, Alan accused me of laziness, furious if I hadn't made dinner. He yelled about the dirty house and laundry.

My obstetrician scheduled a cesarean section because my baby was breech — not in the correct position for delivery. Alan was sober during the procedure but left the hospital a few hours after our son was born. When he returned, I knew he had been drinking. He passed out on the cot in my hospital room. When the baby grew hungry and cried, I paged the nurses for help because my surgical scars prevented me from picking him up myself.

Once Alan, the baby and I returned home, he continued accusing me of not doing enough around the house. While the baby napped one day, Alan asked me to help him clean out the shed in the backyard. I accidentally tripped over the roots of a bush, breaking open an incision. I started bleeding heavily. Alan was drunk, so we loaded the baby into the car seat, and I held a maxi pad over my incision to absorb the blood as I drove to the hospital.

Fortunately, the doctors addressed the problem and stopped the bleeding. Alan, however, left for the liquor store and drove drunk with the baby in the car.

Three months later, Alan and I married in a 10-minute ceremony. I didn't want my son to grow up without his father like I had. There was no pomp and circumstance for this wedding — Alan and I wore street clothes. My best friend held our infant son and watched as we filled out the paperwork.

We vacationed at a cabin in the mountains owned by Alan's dad. Alan and I started arguing when I realized that while I'd been getting groceries, he'd bought a $30 jug of whiskey. In the car, I punched my husband's arm.

"Don't ever hit me again!" Alan stepped out of the car and walked away. I grabbed the whiskey, removed the cap from the jug and threw it out the window into a ditch. When I located Alan, I apologized and asked if he was okay. He refused to speak to me. Back at the cabin, he wanted to know where his whiskey was.

"I threw it out," I admitted.

"What do you mean, you threw it out?"

"I'm not going to deal with you being drunk."

Alan punched me in the face. I ran into one of the bedrooms, but he followed and continued hitting me. I sprinted out the back door and stepped into the snow without shoes. I had left our son asleep inside the cabin. Alan began throwing my clothes and purse outside. I called my best friend.

"Pray for me," I begged. "He's going to kill me."

Alan locked me out of the cabin. I huddled inside our car, trying to get warm. *What am I going to do? I'm in the middle of nowhere. My baby's stuck in the cabin with his angry father.* But after a few hours, Alan let me back inside.

In the morning, we heard a vehicle coming up the driveway. Alan's dad showed up unannounced, wanting to see his grandson. I had a black eye, and Alan told me to hide it using my hair.

About six months after we married, we decided to move to Missouri. *This can be a fresh start for us. Maybe Alan will change.*

At first, we lived in a motel. Then one day at the Laundromat, I met a man who offered to sell us a duplex, and we moved into our new home.

No surprise — Alan didn't change. His co-workers invited him out drinking. I stayed home caring for the baby at first. When Alan came home from the bar, he ripped into me for not doing enough. The house didn't appear as immaculate as he thought it should look. He insisted I find a job and return to work.

When I did, I discovered a new group of friends who wanted to party with me. On nights I hit the bars, I left our son at home with Alan. He'd drink from a bottle from the liquor store.

Also at work, I became friends with a man named Mike who was old enough to be my father. He trained me to operate the forklift and taught me about making good financial decisions, like saving for retirement. Mike was divorced and had a son and daughter about the same age as my brother and me. He didn't have a great relationship with his children, so he took me under his wing. When I would get frustrated or irritable at work, Mike calmed me down.

"It is what it is." Mike repeated those words of wisdom to frequently help me through bad days. His other catchphrase was "unbelievable."

స్వస్వస్వ

I was driving home with my mom and some of her friends we had picked up at the airport. A babysitter was watching my son. When I turned off the highway at the exit for my house, I spotted Alan's car abandoned on the side of the road. *What is he doing?*

I dropped off Mom and her friends and discovered that Alan was not at our house. I made phone calls and drove around looking for him, with no luck. As I pulled in my driveway, I glimpsed a police car creeping down the street. I flagged down the officer.

"Are you looking for me?" I asked.

"Are you Tori?"

"Yes, I am." I sighed. "What has he done now? How drunk is he?"

"Drunk enough that he didn't give me the right home address," the officer replied. He guided me to another police car. Alan sat on the seat, slumped over. The police officer told me that people found him in a nearby field. Apparently his car had run out of gas, so he left it at the exit and tried to walk home.

"Do you want to take him home?" the police inquired.

"No! You take him."

"You want us to take him to jail?"

"Yes. Take him to jail."

Alan stayed in the drunk tank until 3 a.m., when he called to tell me the police were releasing him. I found him walking down our street in the rain without a coat. So I picked him up and brought him home. Later, I found out his boss fired him for drinking too much on the job. That's why he was so intoxicated the day he ran out of gas.

Instead of this incident convincing me to leave Alan, we bought a new house, and I got pregnant with our second child. After the birth of my second son, my 3-year-old began asking me tough questions.

"Why is Daddy mean to you? Why does he yell at you? Why does he hit you?"

One night, I sat in the recliner eating dinner from Taco Bell. Alan started calling me fat and criticizing me for being overweight. He told me I didn't need to eat.

When he left the room, I pursued him and yelled back at him. He pushed me down the hallway, and I fell to the ground, where he kicked me.

"Stop it! Stop it!" our son pleaded.

Alan retreated to our bedroom and closed the door. I rushed to comfort our crying son.

After two pregnancies, I had gained some weight. I had never been skinny, but at that time, I wore a size 20. I started working out and losing weight. I enjoyed hearing people compliment me on my appearance. I spent six days each week at the gym, eventually fitting into a size 10. In public, Alan would put his arm around me and show me off. But at home, he continued to berate me.

People are noticing me. Why am I still married to Alan? Surely someone else will love me. If not, losing this weight proves that I can set a challenging goal and work hard to accomplish it. I can take care of myself and my boys.

I finally mustered up the courage to tell Alan our marriage was over. Initially, he didn't react strongly. I moved out with the kids. Two months later, on our four-year anniversary, his phone call woke me up around 7 a.m. The co-worker I had started dating had spent the night with me.

"I'm going back to California," Alan announced. "If I can't have you and the boys, then I'm not staying here."

Before I knew it — almost a week later, on Christmas — machines were keeping Alan alive. I traveled to California and watched him die. When I returned to work after the trip, Mike didn't say a word when he saw me. He held out his arms and hugged me. I sobbed into his shoulder for a long time.

తతత

I ate from a bag of chocolate chip cookies on the passenger seat next to me. Soon the bag was empty. My stomach churned afterward, and I forced myself to throw up the food.

I binged and purged after Alan's suicide. I thought

food would make me feel better. But after overeating, I only felt worse.

I blamed myself for screwing up my relationship with Alan so badly, and I vowed never to marry again. I wanted to be alone for a change. I withdrew from George, the co-worker I had started dating.

Alan's life insurance didn't cover his death since it wasn't an accident. I sold his Jeep and pickup truck, as well as the two houses we owned, to pay off thousands of dollars in credit card debt. After that, I didn't have much money left to support myself and my kids. I had never gone very long without a man in my life, either. So we moved into George's place, which felt like a safe haven where no one would judge me. George had horses, and the boys and I loved brushing them — it was relaxing.

One of my aunts invited us to attend a service at a new church called LifePoint that was meeting in a funeral home. The first Sunday I visited, George was working. Men at the church greeted me warmly and shook my hand. I regarded them skeptically, since almost all the men in my life had mistreated me. I soon realized, however, that the people at LifePoint genuinely cared about others.

Another Sunday, George and I sat next to each other as "Amazing Grace" played at the end of the service. I sang with my eyes closed, thinking about how much God loved me. I had spent my life turning to alcohol, pot, food, popularity, material possessions and sex to cover up the pain in my heart from the pain I endured, beginning with my father. None of those escapes had worked. Singing that song, tears streamed down my face, and strong emotions overwhelmed my body. George and I made eye contact, and I realized he felt strange, too.

We both walked forward and found a place to pray. "How precious did that grace appear the hour I first believed," everyone sang. *God, I believe what I really need in life is your unconditional love. Your amazing grace means you forgive me for all the mistakes I've made. I can barely grasp the fact that Jesus died and rose again so that I could be free of guilt and shame. I give my life to you, Lord.*

After the music ended, my uncle hugged George and me. Grabbing the microphone, he introduced us to the church and announced that we would be getting married soon because we wanted to please God, whose plan is that sex be reserved for marriage. We continued attending church faithfully and making new friends at LifePoint.

A few months later in the fall, I dressed in a chocolate-brown gown for our wedding at the hitching post outside George's barn. Our guests, including many people from LifePoint, sat on bales of hay. My sons and I arrived riding the tractor. George wore jeans and cowboy boots. Our boss from work performed the ceremony. At the reception, we served hot dogs, chili and corn on the cob.

George wanted all four of us to have the same last name, and he wished to make a lifelong commitment to loving my boys as their father. He legally adopted them, and we officially became a family. But we desired to have a child of our own as well.

When I didn't get pregnant right away, I felt frustrated. A friend of mine suggested that maybe God wanted me to address some of my past issues before having another baby.

I easily made some changes after dedicating my life to God. Before we even started attending LifePoint, my older son once questioned me about cooking chicken with beer. He pointed to the beer cans in the refrigerator.

"What is that?"

"That's alcohol," I replied. "You can't drink that."

"That's why Daddy died. Why do we have that?"

My son's observation stunned me. I removed all the alcohol from the house. From that day forward, I never had another drink.

I tried to obey the Lord. Yet I clung to the deep-seated hatred I felt toward my father. I believed God wanted me to forgive people who had wronged me, but the hurt I still bore from my father's abuse seemed to be too much to forgive. I wanted to ignore it and put it behind me.

Celebrate Recovery is a Biblically based 12-step program offered at LifePoint for anyone with "a hurt, habit or hang-up." George and I attended Celebrate Recovery together each week. As I completed the steps and dealt with my past, it helped strengthen our marriage.

First, I had to "realize I'm not God. I'm powerless to control my tendencies to do the wrong things, and my life has become unmanageable." I decided to give God control over how I felt about my dad. But that wasn't a one-time decision. Every day, I must give control to the Lord.

Second, I needed to "earnestly believe that God exists, that I matter to him and that he has the power to help me recover." *I matter to God? Even though men have made me feel like I have no value, God really cares about me.*

Third, I worked to "consciously choose to commit my life and will to Christ's care and control." I realized Jesus wanted me to stop hating my father and forgive him instead, even if I didn't ever want to have a relationship with him.

Fourth, I had to "openly examine and confess my faults to myself, to God and to someone I trust." For a long time, I believed I deserved to be treated badly. Through Celebrate Recovery, I learned I wasn't perfect but that I wasn't to blame for all the times I was hurt.

The final step was to "yield myself to God to be used to bring the good news to others, both by example and by my word." I needed to begin teaching others about God, particularly my children. The Celebrate Recovery process successfully freed me from my past.

えええ

At work, Mike bade me farewell for the weekend. He planned to take a week of vacation.

"Try to behave yourself." He loved to tease me. "Don't get yourself fired. You better be here when I get back."

I gave him a hug and, strangely, didn't want to let go. We clocked out and walked to our cars in the parking lot.

The following Monday, a friend called me.

"Have you spoken to Mike?"

"No. Why?"

"You need to call his girlfriend and find out what's going on," my friend warned.

I left a message on his girlfriend's phone, and she finally called me back. They had stopped at a casino in Minnesota. While eating dinner, Mike choked on a piece of steak. Someone performed the Heimlich maneuver, but it failed to dislodge the food. The paramedics found that the piece of steak punctured his lung. They resuscitated him, but he had been without oxygen for too long. He had no brain function and was on life support.

I couldn't believe it. Mike had treated me like his daughter. He was the closest person in my life to a father. Machines kept him alive at a hospital too far away for me to visit him. His girlfriend and children kept him on life support for about a week. When they turned off the machines, Mike lived about 10 minutes. Then he died.

At the visitation, I silently studied the photos on display. When Mike's girlfriend saw me, she embraced me and began introducing me as one of Mike's closest friends. I met his daughter for the first time, and she hugged me, too.

"I know how much my dad loved you. I'm so sorry he's gone."

Until that moment, I never knew that Mike told other people about me. His girlfriend invited me to sit with the family at the funeral. I cried hard when the speaker mentioned my name during the eulogy. "Unbelievable." I could hear Mike's voice clear as day. "Unbelievable."

I turned to the Lord for comfort as I grieved for Mike. I felt God with me, helping me through the devastation of the unexpected loss. I concentrated on being grateful for the time I had shared with Mike.

෭෭෭

I finally became pregnant after three years of marriage to George. God was blessing us with a little girl! I developed gestational diabetes, and then an ultrasound showed that the placenta attached too deeply to the wall of my uterus — a condition known as placenta accreta.

The doctors would try to separate the placenta and uterus during my cesarean. If they couldn't, they would need to perform a hysterectomy. There was a risk I could bleed to death. My doctor prayed with me, and Pastor Kelly from LifePoint prayed with George and me. We decided to schedule the hysterectomy along with the cesarean.

Because of my high-risk pregnancy, I underwent ultrasounds weekly. After 36 weeks, the images showed the baby wasn't being nourished properly. The doctors scheduled my surgery for the next day, which happened to be April Fool's Day. We asked LifePoint to put me on the prayer list.

In the delivery room, I felt excited to meet my baby girl. She looked perfect when they pulled her out of the womb, even though she only weighed 4 pounds, 15 ounces. George cradled her in his arms.

Suddenly, pain shot through my body. The nurses and doctors scurried around the room.

I cried as feeling returned to my legs — the anesthesia had worn off. They placed a mask over my face, and I fell asleep.

The placenta had not only endangered my uterus, but also my bladder. The surgical team worked hard to save my bladder. While I was in surgery, many people prayed for me.

In recovery, I continued to feel intense pain, and medicine didn't help much. An ambulance rushed my daughter to a hospital an hour away with a neonatal intensive care unit. Her lungs hadn't developed enough before her birth.

I remained hospitalized for three days. Finally, the doctors released me, and I headed straight to the NICU to see my daughter.

We stayed at a Ronald McDonald House, watching our baby gain weight and develop stronger lungs in the hospital over the next 10 days.

I stayed home from work for 12 weeks so that I could fully heal from my surgery and take care of our precious gift from God. People from LifePoint brought meals to our home for eight weeks so that I wouldn't be bothered with cooking.

Ever since then, when I gaze at my healthy daughter, I think of the words to a song we sing in church: "You make beautiful things out of the dust. You make beautiful things out of us."

UNBROKEN

God transformed my life — the years of abuse, my father's absence and Alan's suicide — into something beautiful. Heartache and death no longer rule me. I know I'm loved as God's beautiful child.

TERMINATION POINT
THE STORY OF KIMBERLY
WRITTEN BY SHELLEY JEAN LOWERY

My husband, Justin, slowed the vehicle as we neared the intersection and scanned the neighborhood. He surveyed the area for anything that resembled a medical facility.

"I don't think this is right," he said with concern.

"This looks more like 'the hood' than a place where a medical clinic would be located."

I heard hushed conversations going on in the backseat but couldn't make out what my mom, dad and twin sister were whispering about.

Then Mom spoke up. "No, this is correct. It's there on the left."

I could hear the anxiety in her voice, and I turned my head to see the weatherworn building that she indicated. The clinic's sign came into view.

It certainly didn't look like the professional-looking building I'd expected. After all, my doctor in St. Louis made this appointment.

Sick to my stomach all morning, I thought, *I will surely vomit.* Sadness, mixed with morning sickness, overwhelmed me. I was glad when Justin finally pulled into the parking lot and turned off the engine.

Sitting back in our seats, we exhaled together. Like

we'd all been holding our breath. We sat for a long moment. Saying nothing. Doing nothing. I felt the tension in the vehicle as we all just stared at the building. And the sign.

Abortion clinic.

I replayed the doctor's words in my head, "This is a clinic where you can discuss your final options."

He didn't use the words "abortion clinic." I guess, in so many words, that is what he said without actually saying it. Justin and I must have been so overwhelmed by the doctor's dire prognosis for our baby's future that we didn't fully realize this next appointment was intended to terminate our pregnancy.

It seemed odd to me that Justin parked a good distance from the building. Normally, he would pull me right up to the door.

Then I saw all the people gathered outside of the building.

They were Right to Life protestors, and we couldn't enter the building without going past them.

What did we get into?

౷౷౷

Justin and I were sweethearts in high school. We started dating when I was 15 and Justin was 16. We were both twins. Twins make up about one out of every 100 births — and the odds are very good that many of the other 99 have secretly wondered what it would be like to be part of a twin-duo. Or better yet, what it would be like to date a twin. We heard every joke in the book about twins, and with us both being twins, that made it even funnier to people. It made for interesting community gossip, for sure.

Living in Lebanon, Missouri, gave us the benefits of a small town. A town that felt like family but was also big enough to afford the comforts of the city. Some people hated the fact that everyone in Lebanon knew your business, but it never bothered me. I just felt like we were one big happy family. And I liked that.

Dating Justin was easy. Twins are used to being in a relationship from birth, so we learned early on how to make compromises in our relationship. I saw that in Justin — he was easy to get along with. Twins are also team players, and we don't know what it's like to be fully alone in the world. I was always a partner with my twin, Kathleen, so when Justin and I began dating, he and I naturally became a team, too. That's not to say there weren't some bumps in the road, but I believe we were both well equipped from birth to be great spouses.

We married a year out of high school, and we loved the idea of having a family. Even while still in high school, we talked about having children. Justin, more than anything else, wanted a Daddy's girl — a little girl that he could spoil rotten. He even picked out a name.

༺༝༝༝

I found out I was pregnant at eight weeks, and Justin and I were both elated. Our obstetrician in Lebanon gave us the option of going to Rolla for our ultrasound. Dr. Shelby said they had more up-to-date facilities and equipment. Of course, we didn't mind driving a few extra miles. We scheduled our appointment for 20 weeks. And when it was time, we drove every mile to Rolla with happy expectation.

It turned out that our first ultrasound was a bust. The baby's legs were folded, and the nurse said the baby was being "timid" and wouldn't show us if it was a girl or a boy. We were disappointed that we came home not knowing the sex of the baby, but we were happy to hear that the heart rate was good and the baby seemed healthy. We were scheduled to return in two weeks to try again.

Returning to Rolla two weeks later, the nurse again asked me to lie on the table and expose my "baby bump." She squeezed a warm jelly out of a tube and onto a wand, called a transducer, and slowly moved it over my belly. She watched the screen and took photos as she went. Justin stretched forward to try to discern what he could see on the screen.

"I bet it's a girl!" he said, looking at me with excitement.

The nurse smiled at him. She then wiped my belly clean with a towel and excused herself, saying, "Dr. Smith will be right in to see you. He will discuss the results of your ultrasound with you."

We talked giddily about the future of our family once

the nurse stepped out of the room. I raised myself up on my elbows and repositioned myself. Laying flat on my back had gotten increasingly difficult. It put too much pressure on my back, and I expected that this discomfort would increase throughout the third trimester of pregnancy. Honestly, I didn't mind. I was going to have a baby! It was worth it. Justin gingerly leaned over me and kissed my forehead as he held my hand. He was happy, too, and we smiled at each other.

Dr. Smith knocked softly on the door and entered before we could respond. He politely introduced himself and said, "Well, let's see if this little munchkin is going to be shy today like last time."

He placed jelly on the transducer just as the nurse had done, and he began rolling it across my big belly. He watched the screen while we excitedly watched him.

Justin impatiently asked, "Well? Boy or girl? Or twins?"

Dr. Smith didn't say anything. He just kept rolling the wand over my belly and going back to a spot on my right side and rolling it over and over and taking pictures with the computer. We could see the concern on his face when he finally swiveled around in his chair.

"I've never seen anything like this in all my years of medical practice," he said.

I felt Justin tighten his grip on my hand. My pulse instantly accelerated, and I got a lump in my throat. I looked at him and waited. Justin, on the other hand, tried to make light of it.

"What are you saying, Doc? Are we having quadruplets instead of twins?"

"No, son. Your baby is missing the lower part of its spine."

During the next half hour, Dr. Smith searched the Web looking for information. It felt like an eternity as we sat in silence as he researched. Satisfied with his results, he turned around and looked at us.

"Your baby has a rare condition called Caudal Regression Syndrome. During pregnancy a baby's spine will grow for eight to 10 weeks. After that, the spine cannot and does not grow," he said. "For some reason, your baby's spine did not complete its growth. The lower half of your baby's spine is missing. Your baby will be lucky to make it through the pregnancy, and if it does, it will never be able to leave the hospital. It probably won't live more than two weeks. I'm a pro-life doctor, but I suggest that you terminate this pregnancy. I'm sorry."

We could not believe what we were hearing. We held onto each other as we made our way back to our vehicle with a fist full of paper printouts about Caudal Regression Syndrome. Justin opened my door to help me into the car and closed the door.

He got in on the driver's side and closed the door.

We both broke down and cried.

∽∽∽

"How can this be happening to us?" I sobbed. Justin held my hand while trying to comfort me. Neither of us could fight off the torrent of emotion that engulfed us as we sat in our vehicle. It overtook us like an unexpected storm. Only an hour prior, we had been filled with joy and excitement, but our euphoria was displaced by fear, confusion and hopelessness.

Those final words of the doctor repeated themselves over and over in my mind like a stuck record: *I suggest you terminate this pregnancy. I'm sorry.*

I'm sorry? I'm sorry you're having this baby? I'm sorry your baby is broken?

Hopelessness is a terrible thing. It will take you to the depths of despair and hold you under, drowning you in defeat. It felt as though we were gasping for air. As tears poured from our eyes, we told each other that it was going to be okay, and we made the decision to talk to our regular physician and to also get a second opinion.

"Perhaps," we told each other, "this was just a big mistake."

ॐॐॐॐ

We talked to Dr. Shelby and told her the bad news about the baby. We told her we wanted a second opinion. She immediately scheduled us for an appointment at Barnes Hospital in St. Louis. Unfortunately, we would have to wait out the weekend — our appointment wasn't until Tuesday.

We agonized as we waited. Friends and family kept calling and asking about the results of the ultrasound and whether we were having a girl, a boy or twins. It was awful. Every time I tried to talk about what was happening to our baby, I cried.

I felt myself slowly building a wall around myself. My hedge of protection, so to speak. I didn't want to talk about what was happening with the baby. In fact, I didn't want to think about it. I decided I needed to go back to work for a couple of days just to give myself something to do. My mind needed to be occupied with something other than the doctor's final words.

We were under a great deal of pressure to make a decision about terminating our pregnancy because of state laws on late-term abortions. Legally, in the state of Missouri, an abortion could not be performed after 23 weeks of pregnancy. That meant we had exactly one week to make our decision. We had always said we would never get an abortion. We had grown up believing that it was a choice we would never make.

I struggled with the fragility of our precious baby. Hopelessness and fear waged a war in my thoughts. It was easy to say, "I will never have an abortion," when sitting around a church table with a cup of coffee and a donut in hand. It was something completely different when a medical doctor told me that my baby would never stand up. And in all probability would never live to even see the outside of the hospital. I felt overwhelmed by the circumstances and the decision that had to be made.

Overwhelmed because it felt like the choice had already been made for me. And that left me with "no choice."

ॐॐॐ

Gray clouds hung like thick curtains across the sky as a drizzling rain misted everything under its cover. Gloom settled on the day, like clouds blotting out the light of day.

It's the perfect day to be carrying the weight of bad news, I thought. *It's as though all creation can feel the heaviness of my heart.*

Kathleen, Mom and Dad came with Justin and me as we again went through all the procedures of another ultrasound. Medical staff determined that we were having a little girl. We met with more doctors, and they confirmed that our little girl definitely had Caudal Regression Syndrome. They explained that the lower part of the spine is what controls the legs and that because she had no lower spine, she would be paralyzed.

"Assuming your baby makes it through the entire pregnancy and delivery, she will never live past a couple of weeks. She will not be able to come home with you from the hospital," the doctor said. "If you continue with the pregnancy, you need to know what the end results will be. I'm so sorry, but terminating this pregnancy is your best option, and you need to do it within the next three days."

ॐॐॐ

We all sat together in the vehicle and stared across the parking lot at the abortion clinic. I tried to push my emotions down while at the same time gathering up my courage to open the car door. Mom and Dad, Kathleen and Justin all waited patiently for me to make the first move. Then I felt a hand on my shoulder as my twin sister leaned forward from the backseat.

"It's going to be okay, Kimberly. I don't know how it's going to be okay, but it's going to be okay," she said lovingly.

I had been fortified until that moment. Holding back the tears. Vowing to be strong. Yet, for some reason, the touch of my twin sister's hand on my shoulder and the sound of her loving voice melted my resolve. I cried.

I had always felt blessed to be a twin. Kathleen and I had been as close as two sisters could possibly be. So close that we often could feel what one another was feeling. And at that moment, I hoped she couldn't feel the wrenching of my heart as all my faith and hope for the child growing inside me got snuffed out like a candle.

Kathleen had taken the day off of work to be by my side, as had Mom and Dad and Justin. I didn't feel alone, and that gave me tremendous comfort.

When that day began, we had not realized where we'd been referred to. Until that moment, we had not realized this was the place where our baby's life would be terminated. And that overwhelmed us.

As we crossed the parking lot to the clinic, I braced myself for coming face to face with the Right to Life protestors at the entrance. We walked together: Mom and Dad, Kathleen, Justin and I. We'd take the protesters on together.

"Please don't abort your baby," a middle-aged woman begged me as I passed her.

Justin tried to protect me and be polite at the same time, pushing her away gently. Another woman tried to persuade us to turn around and not go inside. *Believe me, that is exactly what I want to do,* I wanted to scream. Not necessarily at them but just scream. *You don't understand! We have to terminate this pregnancy. We don't have a choice!*

We were all emotionally shaken by the time we made it past the protesters and into the waiting room of the clinic. A nurse immediately separated me from my family, even Justin, and had me go alone into another room to fill out the paperwork. The nurse said I needed to be alone so I would not be influenced by anyone in the family — even my husband.

Yes, I could make my own decisions. I was a strong enough woman to do so. However, to be taken from my twin sister, my mother and father, and my husband left me trembling. I tried to fill out the paperwork, but I was shaking so hard that I couldn't seem to put pen to paper. I had this terrible feeling in the core of my being that just wouldn't allow me to calm down. I then felt my phone vibrate, and I took it out of my purse and looked at it. It was Justin.

"Please, come out to the front waiting area! NOW!"

I gathered my belongings and headed out the door to find my husband. I was so glad to feel his arms around me and know that I was not alone in this decision. He held me close for a brief moment and then held me at arm's length so he could look me in the eyes.

"Kimberly, we can't do this. We can't do this to our little girl. I finally got my little girl, and we can't give up on her."

"Yes!" I immediately concurred. "We cannot do this to our little girl!"

Mom, Dad and Kathleen could hear us from the rooms they had been waiting in. We each had been separated into different rooms — divided by walls. Yet, each one of us prayed to God and asked for help. As Mom and Dad and Kathleen waited in their respective rooms, they each felt the same uneasiness about the abortion, and one by one, they stepped out of hiding to find Justin and me.

As we came together in the hallway, we discovered that walls were no match for the bond that we shared as a family, nor were they a barrier to our prayers for help. We were in agreement — aborting the growing life inside me was the wrong choice.

As we quickly exited the building, we made our way through the small crowd of protesters. The same woman who had begged me not to abort my baby looked at me with compassion and said, "God bless you for giving your baby a chance to live."

Walking toward the vehicle, my dad stopped and

began to weep. It was the first time I had ever seen my father openly cry. The experience was difficult for all of us.

Pulling out of the parking lot, I noticed a small parting in the cloud cover. I leaned forward in my seat for a better view and looked at it with anticipation. There amongst the dark luminous clouds was a single ray of light laboring to break through. The darkness tried but could no longer hold back the light, and the sunbeam shot through the darkness, making its grand escape.

I leaned back in my seat as tears began to form and roll down my cheeks. It probably meant nothing to anyone else who saw it. But to me, it felt like a kiss from heaven. A symbol of light conquering darkness. Despair overtaken by hope. A sign from God saying, *Thank you, Kimberly, you did the right thing.*

We certainly didn't know what the future held for our little girl, but we trusted that God held her future.

❧❧❧

During the next few months, we went to dozens of doctor appointments to monitor the progress of our baby girl. I drove to St. Louis every two weeks to have MRIs, echocardiograms and non-stress tests. It was decided that I would have the baby by Cesarean section, and we scheduled it for 39 weeks of pregnancy.

The hospital arranged for us to have a full tour of the hospital. This would not be an ordinary birth, and they wanted us to know what to expect on delivery day. When we arrived, they showed us where the operation would take place, where the recovery room was and the NICU where our baby girl would stay.

The neurologist, urologist and surgeon met us in a conference room and introduced themselves to Mom and Dad, Kathleen, Justin and me. Then Dr. Simmons, the neurologist, showed us pictures of our baby's spine taken from the MRI. He showed us how her legs were crossed. "They will stay that way because they are paralyzed."

Dr. Hopkins, the urologist, said, "The lower spine controls the bladder and kidneys, and until she gets older, we won't know how much control she will have over these functions."

I looked over at Justin, as if to say, "Did he say, 'When she gets older'? How can he be talking about her getting older when she won't live past two weeks?"

"Wait! Hold on. Are you saying that our baby girl is going to live?" Mom leaned forward begging a response. And we all waited.

Dr. Hopkins looked at us with confusion.

"We have been told that she will not live. We've been told that she would not leave the hospital and go home!"

Kathleen raised her voice in excitement. "Are you telling us that this is not true?"

Dr. Hopkins looked at the other two doctors and then back at us and asked, "Who told you that?"

Justin exclaimed, "The doctors at THIS hospital!"

"Well, I don't know why they told you that, but your little girl will be okay. You will get to take her home. She will need extra doctor appointments so we can monitor her development, but she is going to do great things!"

We could not believe what we were hearing! This was the first good news we'd heard about our baby girl's future.

చచచ

In a few weeks, we held a baby shower for the baby — something that we hadn't felt like planning before. We also prepared a nursery for our sweet baby girl to come home to. I worked long and hard on the nursery.

One night, I'd been decorating with items I received at the baby shower, and I clumsily lowered my pregnant body into the rocking chair to rest for a moment. Leaning back, I looked at the space above the crib and imagined painting Mattea's name on the wall above it. Mattea, the name that Justin and I had chosen for our little girl way back in high school. Back before we were pregnant. Before we were even married.

A name lodged in our hearts.

I wonder what Mattea means, I thought to myself. I reached for my cell phone and searched for the meaning of her name. Tears filled my eyes as I read it. Mattea means "gift of God."

చచచ

Soon, I gave birth to our baby girl, our gift from God. At 5 pounds, 2 ounces, she was stable, breathing on her own, alert and responding well. We brought her home 20 days later, on Father's Day.

৯৯৯

Justin and I sipped coffee with our sister-in-law, Sharon. We watched Mattea move around the room using her arms and hands. Because of her spinal condition, Mattea's legs are permanently crossed. But she learned very quickly to get around, anyway. She could probably beat me in a race!

Full of life and joy, she played with her myriad of toys — gifts from grandparents who love her. We watched her with awe as her blond curls bounced and blue eyes sparkled.

I can't imagine life without her. I smiled to myself.

Sharon got up and poured herself another cup of coffee and came back to sit on the couch with me, while Justin played with Mattea on the floor.

"It's wonderful," she said.

"What's wonderful?"

"How much God loves Mattea." Sharon smiled. "It seems to me that God gifted you with his precious little Mattea. He placed her in your care because he trusted you with her."

"How so?" Justin spoke up.

"You two are the perfect choice for Mattea. Think

about it. Even your hobbies are things that Mattea can participate in. Imagine how difficult it would be if your hobbies were things like mountain climbing or hunting. It's just so amazing to me!"

"Hmmm. I never thought of that," I said as I glanced over at Mattea and Justin as they played with Mattea's pastel Lego blocks.

"And," she continued, "working for the school district gives me the knowledge and insight to help you know what will be available for Mattea in school. Aunt Sue and your sister, Kathleen, are both nurses and can help with the medical terminology and physical issues that arise."

Justin added, "And Grandma crochets all of Mattea's shoes to fit her club feet!"

We laughed, but it was true.

"Our whole family is perfect for Mattea," Sharon said. "You will never have to get a babysitter or need to send her to daycare."

"No!" I almost shouted. "And she never will. Our parents fight over who gets to watch her next."

"Isn't it wonderful that both sets of grandparents live just a couple of blocks away?" Sharon took another drink of her coffee. "Mattea is God's gift to you. But YOU are also God's gift to Mattea."

∽∽∽

It's hard to believe we nearly terminated Mattea's life. That words like "I'm sorry" and "hopeless" were ever associated with such a beautiful little girl. I understand that for many people, the thought of raising a child with a handicap or syndrome is too burdensome to bear. So they make the heartbreaking choice, perhaps also following their doctors' advice, to take matters into their own hands. As we came so close to doing ourselves.

What we learned to trust through our experience is that God is sovereign, and he is also good. As parents, we can rest in the full knowledge of his character and his promises. We saw that God does not abandon us, his children, leaving us to make these decisions on our own. He stays near.

We also learned that children — all children — are a blessing from God. We are so glad we made the choice to trust God with Mattea's life, regardless of what that might look like. The joy and blessing she has brought to our lives is beyond measure. True to her name's meaning, Mattea is our "gift from God."

BEGIN AGAIN
THE STORY OF CHRIS
WRITTEN BY KAREN KOCZWARA

"You are not taking those boys!" Heidi screamed.

"You have your boyfriend and your needles," I retorted.

She jumped up and tried to kick me. I'd been taught to never hit a woman, but I was truly afraid of my wife. I grabbed her leg and pulled her onto the couch.

"Don't you dare take those boys!" she screamed, charging after me.

I ran from her, throwing the coffee table in her path. As she got closer, I knocked the kitchen table and chairs over as well, hoping to buy a couple seconds. I raced outside and jumped into the borrowed car. Just as I jammed the key in the ignition, Heidi appeared at the passenger door, her eyes fiery with rage.

Heart thudding in my chest, I pressed the gas pedal and sped off, driving far, far away.

I'll hunt you down and kill you. Her words pounded through my mind with each passing mile.

Please, just go away, Heidi. Don't look for me. Just let me start my life over, once and for all.

৵৵৵

I was born in Tulsa, Oklahoma. My mother was just 15 and my father 17 when they first met. A year later, my mother learned she was pregnant with me. Upon my birth, they moved into a little trailer, married and tried to make a life. But that life proved tumultuous from the start.

I don't remember much about my early years, except for all the yelling and fighting. My mother often lashed out at my father. He lashed out in return, and I got caught in the middle. When I was 4 years old, they parted ways and divorced.

I moved in with my mother in the projects in North Tulsa. It was not the nicest place, and I was one of the few white kids in the neighborhood. My mother struck up a relationship with a new guy. She received stamps from the government to purchase merchandise at the local store, and her guy stole them and sold them for crack. Divorced, with three daughters of his own, this man became violent, the drugs getting the best of him. One day, he came to me and said goodbye.

"I really do love you and think the world of you, but I've got to go," he said. And just like that, he was off, heading toward Colorado to start a new life.

My mother moved us to another apartment and signed a six-month lease. When that place didn't work out, we moved again. She landed a job at a local Arby's and began dating the general manager. They married, but much like her relationship with my father, that one dissolved as well.

As a young, single parent, my mother took out her stress on me. When I got in trouble, she resorted to physical and emotional abuse. I spent every other weekend at my father's house, which felt a bit more stable. He was living the single, partying lifestyle and spent much of his time at the drag-racing strip. I hung around the strip with him, trying to fit into his world, but I felt more like an outsider looking in. He'd found a woman and gotten remarried. She had a 2-year-old daughter he'd adopted, and after marrying, they had another little girl. His new wife was very manipulative. She fake cried and accused me of hurting her. To avoid conflict and confrontation, my father hung out in his large vegetable garden, where he found solace. They eventually divorced.

My mother divorced her second husband, and we moved again, this time into another apartment in Tulsa. I met a guy named Scout in the complex, and we became fast friends. It's hard to make friends when you're constantly moving, and I valued my friendship with Scout.

One day, I learned he had a brain tumor. Just a kid, I didn't understand all the implications of the horrible disease, but I was afraid he might die.

Scout's mother, especially protective, discouraged our boyish roughhousing.

"Scout needs his rest," she reminded us.

My mother worked two jobs and went through a string of new boyfriends. None of them seemed to last long. I spent most of my time with Scout, the one constant, positive person in my life. One day, my mother's ex-boyfriend came back from Colorado and turned up at a grocery store where she was shopping.

"I'm gonna get you both," he threatened.

My mother, frightened by his violent temperament, decided to get out of Tulsa, once and for all. She moved us to Wichita, Kansas, where we started over once again. I began the sixth grade, and she found work as an escort. She met yet another guy, and he eventually became her third husband.

Unlike the others, he took on the role of a real stepfather, and I liked him well enough. But life didn't get any easier. Scout died that winter, and I grieved the best friend I'd ever known. By junior high, I'd learned all about gangs, and I began fighting. It seemed the only way to avoid getting trampled was to join the crowd.

When I turned 13, my mother asked if I wanted to live with my father full time. She and her new husband were getting on well, and it seemed they wanted a life of their own. Considering life was getting pretty rough around Wichita, I figured moving back to Oklahoma might not be such a bad idea.

My father had moved 40 miles west of Tulsa, into a trailer in a little lake town.

My father commuted into Tulsa every day for work. After getting home each evening, he grabbed a few drinks and turned his music up loud. Eventually, he passed out and went to bed. The next morning, he always said, "Tell me when to stop, son!" I'd remind him that I'd tried but that he was already too drunk to listen.

Like my mother, he went through a string of relationships, too. When I turned 14, my father began dating a new girl who'd just graduated high school. She was nearly half his age. She smoked, and I started smoking, too. My father often hit the bars after work, and after having a few too many beers, he crashed at my grandmother's house in town. We were already drifting apart, living our own lives, the distance between us widening.

I met a guy named Josh in the ninth grade, and we started getting drunk together, raiding my father's liquor cabinet here and there. One day, Josh offered me some acid, and I tried it.

"You just put it on your tongue, like this," he said, demonstrating. "It's amazing."

Josh was right. Acid was amazing, unlike anything I'd ever experienced. By age 14, I was smoking, drinking, dropping acid, smoking pot and stealing. In a little town of 7,000 people, with only one stoplight and one gas station, there wasn't much to do.

My friends and I raided people's cars at the local Bingo hall, scouring them for loose change and cigarettes. With our findings, we purchased more pot. We stole bikes and pellet rifles from storage sheds. After a school fundraiser, we unlocked a window, broke into the building and stole the money. We also broke into a church, stealing the Sunday offerings.

One night, my friend and I headed over to the Bingo hall, where we broke in and stole the money bag. After escaping, we counted more than $2,000 in cash. Unable to keep his mouth shut, Josh told his friend Ron, and Ron told his mother. When I learned what he'd done, I panicked.

"We have to leave town," I said. "We're gonna be in huge trouble!" I knew if we got caught, we could face some serious consequences. I was just 15 years old. I didn't want to spend time in juvenile hall. We needed to get out of there and quick.

My friend agreed to the plan. We walked through town, avoiding everyone. We stopped at a house with a storage shed, raiding it for macaroni and cheese and other essentials. We then packed our bags, and when night fell, we made our escape.

We arrived at a local steakhouse, where we scanned the parking lot for a car to steal. We lucked out and found some keys behind the visor in an old Ford pickup truck, and we took off in it, heading toward Tulsa without looking back.

Not far down the road, however, we discovered that the truck was stuck in first gear. My friend tried everything to get it unstuck, but it would not budge. I suggested he put it in neutral, but he didn't listen. We overheated the truck near a bar outside of town.

We tried hot-wiring another car, but a guy ran out into the parking lot, scaring us away.

It was a chilly October night, and I knew we wouldn't last long if we didn't get somewhere warm soon. We trudged into the woods and started a fire. In the morning, we decided to hitchhike into Tulsa. Not long after heading down the road, I spotted a sheriff's vehicle up ahead.

"That's a sheriff," I hissed to my friend, pointing at the car.

"Just be cool," he said. "We're just a couple of 15-year-old boys, walking down the highway, minding our own business."

But to my dismay, the sheriff turned around and pulled up beside us. Our parents had filed missing persons reports, and the cops had been looking for us ever since. The sheriff hauled us back to town, and I prepared to face my father, afraid he'd be furious. My father and I weren't especially close, but I knew he still loved me and wanted me safe. I'd never gotten into any sort of real trouble before. What sort of punishment lay ahead?

My dad was waiting for me at the station. I broke down in tears, horrified that I'd let him down. The cops interviewed me and my friend, asking if we'd had any involvement in stealing some sound equipment from a church.

"I did not do that. I'm telling you the truth, sir," I said, pleading with the cop to believe me.

The cops let me off with a warning that day, but Josh went to juvy. My father took me all around town to apologize to everyone I'd wronged. The owner of the truck was waiting in the parking lot. We apologized for stealing his vehicle. "I think we burned up your transmission," I confessed.

"That transmission is built for a Thunderbird," he said. "You should have put the truck in neutral." His reaction surprised me. I was sure I'd be dead meat.

I returned to school, where I continued getting into trouble. Ron and I became friends, and I began hanging out with him and his two friends, Jana and Jeff. Their father was an alcoholic, and his fridge was always stocked with Coors Light. We snatched a few here and there, trekked out into the field behind their house and drank our share. We were a small posse, jumping off barn roofs, drinking, looking to pass the time in our small town.

Toward the end of my junior year, my father said we needed to move. He'd been living with a new woman for a while, and their relationship was considered a common law marriage. He sold our trailer to Ron, and we relocated back to Tulsa, leaving our small town behind. I enrolled at the large high school my parents had attended when they were teens. I expected to fit right in, but to my dismay, my peers shunned me.

"You hick hillbilly!" they sneered.

"Don't you remember me? We played soccer and baseball together when we were kids," I reminded them.

But elementary school, it seemed, was a long time ago. They'd forgotten all about me, and I had to make friends all over again.

I started hanging out with the stoners and slackers, smoking pot again. One day, I walked home with one of the girls in the group, and we smoked pot together. She told the other guy in the house to go home, and then we started messing around. The next thing I knew, she handcuffed me to the bed and forced herself on me. I knew she had a reputation for getting around, but I hadn't expected such boldness. I panicked, sure I might get HIV. *What if she told everyone I'd come on to her?* This certainly hadn't been my plan.

In drama class my senior year, I met a guy named Mitch. We hit it off right away, sleeping through English class together. Mitch was a goofy, fun guy, but beneath his jovial exterior lay a very broken kid. His mother was dying of cancer, and he lived off her social security checks, raising his little brother without a father in the picture. Me, Mitch and his brother Ricky became a tight little group.

Mitch got his own apartment and continued living off his mother's social security checks. We hung out every day, getting stoned, drinking and dropping acid. Nothing was off limits.

One night, Mitch and some other friends of ours had a hair-dying party. We got high and then dyed our hair wild colors. I did mine, knowing all the while my father would kill me when he saw it. When I got home that night, my stepmother was still up.

"Your hair looks cool," she said.

I went into my room and hopped on the phone to make a call. When my father walked in, he grew livid. "Son, you get off that phone right now! And your hair better be the right color in the morning!"

I hung up the phone, my heart sinking. The dye was semi-permanent. There was no way it would come out by morning.

I knew I'd pushed all my father's buttons by then. He

was tired of my antics, tired of always keeping track of me. "This is my house, and my rules. You don't like it? Then get out!" he'd said after grounding me a few times.

I was 18. I decided my best bet was to move in with Mitch. I packed my stuff and bunked at his place.

By 5:30 p.m. that evening, my father came looking for me. When I opened the door, I could see that my father was drunk.

"Can I talk to you?" he asked.

I nodded, my heart sinking.

To my surprise, my father didn't lash out. "Son, I don't care what color your hair is. I am proud of you. You're going to be a man."

"Thank you," I muttered, taken aback by his words.

A man, I thought as I closed the door. *Was my father really proud of me?*

My senior year was coming to an end. After I broke up a fight between a white girl and a black girl on a bus one day, the black girl's gang of friends came after me at school. They threatened me, but the school cops broke up the situation before they beat me up. Rattled, I went home that afternoon and decided not to go back to school. I was always high, and half the time I slept through class. *Who needed a diploma, anyway?*

Mitch and I had fun that summer. We became low-level drug dealers, selling quarter sacks of pot. After scoring weed for ourselves, we got high with our apartment managers. With no adult supervision, we decided to live it up. We strung up Christmas lights and slapped some posters on the walls. The trash piled up, as did the dishes. But we ignored it all, usually too high to care. Mitch met a girl, and we all began hanging out. She became pregnant not long after they started dating, and he decided to stick things out with her.

Meth, or crank as we knew it, was a drug I'd never done before, but an hour after trying it, I knew I'd fallen in love. Crank made me feel like I was invincible. It brought out my creative side as well. I began playing the guitar and writing beautiful poetry. It was as if something had been unlocked inside of me. Our lives now revolved around trying to score meth, and soon, it became the center of our world.

My friends and I slipped into dangerous territory, losing ourselves to the drug. We went on two-and-a-half-week binges, not eating or even drinking water. After a long binge, I finally got hungry and decided to eat. Shortly afterward, I passed out. When I awoke, it took me 20 minutes to crawl up the stairs. I slept for two days straight, got up to go to the bathroom and then slept another day. My body began to atrophy, and I felt myself slipping away. I grew frightened, afraid I might really die. In my weakened, half-alert state, I could hardly move or call out for help.

Mitch came to check on me. "You okay, man?" he asked, his eyes widening when he saw me in bed. He looked as scared as I felt.

I forced myself to fall out of bed, then scooted on the floor all the way to the bathroom. Glancing in the mirror,

I gasped at my reflection. My face was covered in sores, and my hair was starting to fall out. I looked and smelled disgusting. Meth was sucking the life out of me, clenching me in its grip, and if I kept it up, I realized I might not get out of bed next time.

Jenny came into my life shortly after that. She was dating one of our friends, and I immediately fell for her. We began hanging out, dealing meth together, and soon, she dumped her boyfriend and started dating me. I decided I loved her, and she professed her love for me. We became unofficially engaged and discussed marriage. I convinced myself Jenny was the best thing to ever happen to me.

My father worked in the printing and graphics business and offered me a job. I learned the trade, grateful for the opportunity. The meth had taken a toll on my body, however. I tried to quit, but I struggled to stay awake at work, nearly falling asleep on the job. Things continued going well with Jenny, and suddenly, I could not imagine life without her.

Jenny's mother worked for a prominent hotel chain and traveled quite a bit. Jenny decided she wanted to help her mother in the business and took off on the road. I missed her terribly. Though I continued working for my father, I realized my life was going nowhere. My parents had been just kids when they had me. I wanted a family of my own — preferably two healthy boys and a wife. I wanted to raise my kids while young and get on with life, like my parents had. I wanted to be with Jenny, but she liked the adventurous life, and I preferred familiar territory. *Could we possibly find middle ground?*

Confused and depressed, I wrote a poem one night. I titled it "Anything But Pray." At 15 years old, I'd attended church, but the experience had left me feeling confused. The church members had started praying and talking in a strange language I did not understand.

Caught up in the moment, I broke down in tears, and they surrounded me and prayed for me. I felt out of place and awkward. I tried the teen Bible study at a church across the street from my school and also attended a few church services on Sunday mornings. But when no one talked to me, I left feeling worse. I then dated a girl who attended church regularly, but when her parents discovered I did not share the same church values, they said, "You're a nice young man, but we want more for our daughter."

As I thought about my experiences with God, I realized I didn't have a very good impression of him or his people. Though I'd fallen into a rut, I didn't think he could pull me out. In fact, I wasn't sure he could do anything for me. As I penned the poem, I cursed God, sneering, "What did he ever do for me?" In my opinion, there was no use wasting any time trying to pray.

I told Jenny I wanted to stay in Tulsa. She was disappointed but understood, and she took off on business again. During a camping trip at a local lake, I met a girl named Heidi. She seemed fun, and I decided I wanted to get to know her better. I cheated on Jenny with her but felt devastated afterward. How could I have done such a thing, betraying the girl I loved?

I confessed to Jenny. "I love you so much, and I want to spend the rest of my life with you," I told her, distraught.

"I forgive you, Chris, but if you do it again, we're done," she said.

"Let's settle down and have a family," I urged her.

But Jenny wasn't ready to do that just yet. Not long after she left, I brought Heidi back to my apartment and cheated on Jenny again. Before Jenny found out through our friends, I decided to tell her myself. I didn't expect her to take me back a second time, but to my surprise, she said, "I'm coming home, Chris. We'll work things out."

Jenny came back to town, and we spent one wonderful night together, trying to work things out. But it soon became clear we were headed in separate directions. She got her stuff and left. Though heartbroken, I knew we could not keep going on that way, being apart, never making any commitments. Jenny and I were officially done.

I started dating Heidi, and before long, I learned she was pregnant. I was going to be a father! As her belly swelled, I secretly hoped for a boy. Heidi and I quit drugs, saying goodbye to meth and cigarettes. I limited my usage to an occasional drink and some pot. I brought in a decent income and decided I could move us into a house on the better side of town. Mitch came to visit, and we hung out with him, his wife and their baby boy. It seemed we were all growing up, turning into responsible adults, finally getting our act together.

Heidi, ever the social butterfly, preferred to be the center of attention at all times. Our house became the party house, and people showed up at all hours of the day and night. I wanted to settle down, to get away from the scene for good, but Heidi didn't seem interested in walking away. She gave birth to our son in November, and we got married. I was thrilled, excited to have a child of my own. I planned to raise him right, to get our lives on track and make a good home for him. But shortly after his birth, our lives began to unravel.

New Year's Eve, Heidi and I went to a huge party. I hadn't done any serious drugs since learning she was pregnant, but with the booze flowing and the music pumping, I began to miss the old scene. By the end of the night, I'd consumed alcohol, smoked and snorted seven different drugs, including pot, alcohol, cocaine, meth, Valium, Xanax and HydroCodone. The rest of the party morphed into a blur, and I had no idea how Heidi and I made it back home. When I awoke in the morning, I felt sick, realizing we were right back where we'd begun.

From then on, Heidi and I immersed ourselves in the hardcore partying world. Our lives became a roller coaster ride of heavy-metal concerts, drugs, sex and pornography. We became mid-level drug dealers, willing to sell anyone anything. Our niche remained pot and meth, but we eventually began selling cocaine. Heidi was a very smart girl and had been offered a scholarship to college. But she had trouble focusing on school and wasn't interested in studying. She preferred to spend her nights getting high and drunk. She sucked me right in, holding me in her grip of manipulation and lies. I loved her, and she was the mother of my son, but I could see we were on a fast track to nowhere.

When Heidi told me she was pregnant again, I breathed a sigh of relief, hopeful that we could settle down and clean up our messy lives. But we didn't. Instead, we partied harder. Heidi disappeared for hours and days at a time, remaining vague about her whereabouts. I stopped asking questions, because I wasn't sure I wanted the answers. Heidi began wearing long-sleeved coats and jackets, and I found this habit suspicious. It was summer, muggy and hot outside. Heidi usually enjoyed showing off her body, donning as little clothing as possible. Why was she wearing long sleeves?

I suspected she was using needles, and my heart sank. I confronted Heidi about it, and she didn't like what I had to say.

"If you are accusing me, I might as well just go off and do those things," she snapped.

Our son Matthew arrived, another beautiful child. The doctors said he was born an addict because of the drugs that had been pumped into his little system during Heidi's pregnancy. My heart twisted in my chest, knowing we'd already given our boy a rough start in this world. I loved him fiercely, but in my gut, I questioned his DNA. *What if this child isn't mine? Heidi is always going here and there, hanging out with people I don't even know. What if she slept with some other guy, and I'm not even the father?* My heart raced at the possibility. I thought of the loser druggies we knew, a few faces coming to mind. *Even if Matthew isn't mine, I know these other guys aren't going to provide him the life he needs. I will raise him as mine, no matter what.*

The minute Heidi had the baby and left the hospital, she returned to her partying ways. I hardly ever saw her, and when I did, she was never sober. When I called her phone, she didn't answer.

I worked 8 to 10 hours per day and tried caring for the boys on my own. In the morning, I rose extra early to dress and feed the boys before heading off to work. When I returned from work, I found Matthew in the same diaper I'd put on that morning. The neighbors stepped in to help, and I appreciated them.

"Your son came over here a few times this week, telling us he was hungry," they told me.

I felt sick, thinking about my boys being neglected while Heidi partied. When she finally did come home, she passed out on the couch, ignoring the boys. She began acting especially secretive, and I suspected she was using needles. Her old boyfriend came to live with us for a while, and we helped him buy a truck. I wasn't thrilled about the idea, but Heidi always had a way of talking me into things. She knew just what to say and how to get her way. I continued going to work, trying to be responsible there, despite her negligence at home. But I was running thin on time and energy and felt ready to snap in two. Something had to give — and soon.

Easter approached, and I told Heidi to meet me at my father's for dinner that Sunday. Three days before Easter, however, she disappeared. On Sunday morning, I cleaned up the boys on my own and headed to my father's, my anger boiling as I drove.

"Where's Heidi?" my father asked when he opened the door.

I was shaking too hard to answer. I walked inside, afraid that if I started talking, I might collapse on that floor and never get up. *I have an addict baby and another son, both of whom are neglected by their mother. I have a wife I never see, who's most likely using needles. My son wanders over to the neighbor's house looking for food. I'm trying to hold it together, going to work and doing the right thing, but I'm at my end here. I can't keep doing this. I'm a total mess and a failure, anything but a man.*

As I cut up the turkey for dinner, I completely mutilated the thing. I hacked it into tiny pieces, my anger rising with every slice of the knife. I considered telling my father about my predicament but decided against it. Once again, my pride got the best of me.

After dinner, I drove around town with the boys, trying to think of somewhere to go. I had the car packed up and wondered if I could just disappear and leave my life behind. I was sinking fast, and I needed a lifeline, a rope to pull me up from the mud. *But was it too late to turn things around?*

When Heidi finally arrived home, I sat her down for a serious talk. "I am nothing but an addict. You are an addict. I don't want to be in this house anymore. I am tired of not having a healthy mother for our boys. I almost left you, but I didn't have anywhere to go," I told her.

Heidi glared at me, her eyes fiery and defensive. "That's right. You have no place to go. You can't leave me. I will hunt you down and kill you."

I stared back at her. I didn't think Heidi was capable of murder, but she wasn't right in the mind. On more than one occasion, I'd come into the room to find the baby in between the bed frame and the mattress, blankets covering his head. I'd shuddered, hoping it was an accident. But with Heidi always high on drugs, one never knew for sure. If her threat was an attempt at manipulation, she'd taken it to a whole new level, and I had no doubt in my mind that she would go after me if I tried to run away.

My mother, who'd moved to California with her new man, returned to Tulsa for my grandmother's wedding. She called me to say she wanted me and the boys there, too. I told Heidi about it, and she insisted our friend Danny come, too. I suspected he was the one shooting Heidi up. Worse yet, I suspected he was also sleeping with Heidi, but I was too afraid to confront her about it.

We decided to camp out in a tent at a nearby campground the weekend of the wedding. That night, Danny offered to inject me with meth, and before I knew it, I found myself saying, "Okay." Moments later, I felt a burn, and I tasted and smelled metal, the sort of taste one might experience if grinding his teeth on hot tin foil. I felt my pupils dilate, and my heart began to race. Danny finished the shot, and I lay down, feeling strange and exhilarated all at once.

This high was completely different than anything I'd ever experienced, and I understood why hardcore users preferred "slamming it" instead of snorting.

I turned to Danny and Heidi and blurted out the words I'd wanted to say for so long. "Are you two having sex?"

They both just stared back at me, not saying yes or no.

Moments later, I heard an undeniable voice from somewhere within me.

If you don't turn back now, there's no hope!

I wasn't sure where it had come from, but I'd heard it loud and clear.

Seconds after that, I puked.

"I'm gonna go shower," I said, standing up. I stumbled to the campground shower, where I tried to sober up. As the warm water trickled down on my shoulders, I stared at the old cement walls, feeling hopeless and lost. I'd reached the lowest point of my entire life. Back in the tent, my wife was probably already messing around with my so-called friend.

I was tired of her calling the shots, tired of watching her traipse around, threatening me and always getting her way. I was tired of living a subpar life, trying to provide for my boys like a single father. Most of all, I was plain tired of being tired.

The high lasted for more than 24 hours. I had to run the camera at my grandmother's wedding, and my hands shook as I tried to steady it and focus. Right then and there, I made up my mind that I was done with drugs — for good. I swore I'd never touch meth again. I did not want anything to do with that drug and its destructive forces. I wanted out and away, once and for all.

My mother, sensing my despair, approached me. "I am taking you and these boys back to California," she said. "I don't know what you are doing, Chris, but this needs to change. I have to go to Wichita for a couple days to be with your grandfather who had a stroke. But when I get back, I'm taking you to California."

"I can't wait, Mom. I need to leave now," I told her, desperation in my voice. "Can I go out to California without you?"

"Okay, I'll call Jim and let him know you're coming," she said.

I dropped the boys off at Dad's house and returned to my house to get our stuff together. I found four credit cards and was surprised to learn they each had high limits. I cleaned out our bank account and packed what I could. I'd figure out the rest when I got to California.

"You take your sorry ass, but you're not taking the boys!" Heidi cried when she realized I was leaving.

"You have your boyfriend and your needles here," I told her. "What more do you need?"

She stood up and tried to kick me. I never believed in hitting a woman, but Heidi had taken kickboxing classes, and I knew she could hurt me if she tried. She tried to kick me, but I grabbed her leg and pushed her onto the couch.

"Don't you dare take those boys!" she screamed.

She jumped up and lunged after me, but I threw a coffee table in her path. As she got closer, I threw other furniture in her path as well. I raced outside, jumping in my friend's little Geo Metro he'd agreed to let me borrow. Just as I turned the key in the ignition, Heidi raced to the side of the passenger door. I sped off, leaving her in the dust. The adrenaline raced through my veins as I pressed my foot to the pedal, grateful to be away from Heidi and her madness.

I picked up the boys and headed west. At last, I stopped in Needles, California. The blazing July sun had just started to set, and the 105-degree heat blasted me as I stepped out of the car. I went into the motel room and turned on the air conditioner, startled to see the room was an unbearable 130 degrees. At last, it cooled off, and I led the boys into the room. I took them into the shower, where we let the cool water cover us. The three of us just sat there, and I began to cry.

"What's wrong, Daddy?" the boys asked, their eyes wide with concern. "Where is Mommy? Is she coming?"

I didn't know how to answer. *How could I tell the boys I never wanted to see their mother again?*

At last, we arrived in Lancaster, California, where my mother and her husband lived. My stepfather welcomed me in, helping me with the boys as my system detoxed for the next two weeks. At last, I regained my energy. July turned into October, and I finally got a job. I called Heidi to let her know where I was and told her to keep the house.

"I'll keep paying the mortgage," I told her.

I worked on getting everything in order, doing exactly what the judge told me to do in order to divorce Heidi. After watching my parents' divorce, I'd told myself I never wanted to go through a divorce of my own. I'd tried everything, giving Heidi every chance in the world. But she'd betrayed my trust time and time again. I could not go back to that old lifestyle. I had to keep moving forward, even if it meant going forward alone.

When I learned our son needed hernia surgery, I told Heidi, and she came out for the procedure. She bunked up at a hotel, and while she was in town, I handed her the divorce papers.

"What the hell is this?" she demanded, staring at the manila envelope in her hands.

But she knew. At last, I could finally get the closure I needed.

After a year, and several hearings, the divorce was finally official. The judge granted me custody of the boys, and Heidi showed little interest in fighting for them. I breathed a sigh of relief, grateful to close that painful chapter of my life and move on. I did not expect an easy life from there on out, but I hoped the worst was behind me. At last, I could offer my boys the life they deserved.

෨෨෨

I enrolled at Antelope Valley Medical College. I worked at Walmart at night to pay the bills. After receiving my diploma, my mother and stepfather decided to relocate to Lebanon, Missouri, and I went with them.

Lebanon is a small town with a big-town feel. I liked it right away. I transferred to another Walmart there, and my mother landed a job at a veterinarian's office. My stepfather watched the boys until I got home from work.

"Where is Matthew?" my mother cried one morning, shaking me awake.

"He's with Jim," I muttered, rubbing the sleep from my eyes.

I glanced out the window, and to my horror, I saw Matthew sitting on the porch alone. My stepfather was gone, and so was my truck. Not long after, we learned he'd been in an accident after he took the truck into town to buy a six-pack of beer. He rolled my truck on the highway and wound up in the hospital. When we arrived at the hospital, he didn't apologize. It was then we realized he'd fallen back into drinking. An alcoholic, he had been closet drinking, and the brutal truth had come out.

My stepfather moved to Wichita, and my mother and I stayed in Lebanon, where I continued raising my boys. Heidi had very little contact, only calling the boys on the holidays. Our new neighbors surrounded us with love and support, giving us hand-me-down clothes for the boys and helping babysit. I watched one couple in particular, blown away by their generosity and genuine love. I learned they went to church.

"We need to get to church," my mother said. "Those boys need a solid foundation."

I wasn't sure what I thought about the idea. I hadn't set foot in church in years and didn't consider myself good enough to go. I still smoked cigarettes, cussed and drank here and there. I was also divorced. I wasn't sure what I thought of God or what he thought of me. *Was it really a good idea for a guy like me to go to church?*

In the end, I decided it was a good idea. My mother was right — my boys needed a good foundation. Though church hadn't left the best taste in my mouth growing up, perhaps it would be different this time. I was willing to give it a second chance.

The moment I walked through those church doors, I sensed something genuine and beautiful in that place. Glancing around, I noticed people seemed connected to one another. They smiled and laughed and seemed to really care. As the pastor shared from the Bible, I felt a familiar sense of warmth. Right then and there, I knew what I'd been missing all along — Jesus.

I'd tried doing things my way for a long time. I'd tried every drug possible. I'd tried alcohol. I'd had my share of one-night stands and meaningless physical relationships. But nothing had filled me up. I'd tried to change on my own, willing myself to do better. But that hadn't worked, either. At the end of the day, I'd only wound up alone, tired and out of resources. I'd come to the end of myself, and I was tired of living a life void of purpose. I wanted peace in my heart instead of strife. I wanted to wake up with hope instead of dread. I wanted a fresh start. And I knew Jesus was the only way to a better life. More importantly, he was the only way to an eternal life. Someday, my trials on earth would pass away, but if I invited him into my life, I could hope to spend eternity with him in heaven. That was the best news of all.

Growing up, I'd used God as an escape hatch, calling on him only in time of need. Then I'd decided I didn't need him at all, that praying was a worthless idea. I'd never really found my place at church, and eventually, I'd given up. But that day, I'd seen something different, something real. I wanted Jesus as a friend and a guide. I wanted what my neighbors and these other folks in church had — a genuine warmth, love and joy I hadn't witnessed in a long time. I was ready to turn my heart over to God.

I prayed that day, asking Jesus to come into my life, confessing the wrong I'd done. "I know I need you, God," I prayed. "I can't do this life on my own. I need you as my Savior. Please forgive me and help me to be a better man. I want you to lead from now on."

A sense of peace washed over me, and I felt wonderful, knowing I'd just made the best — and most important — decision of my life. I still had a long way to go, still had addictions to break and bad habits to kick. But this time, I did not feel like I faced them alone. I had God on my side, and I trusted that he would help me conquer anything in my path. With his strength, I'd find my way.

෨෨෨

As I stood in church, raising my hands and praying, I remembered being 15 years old in that church years before, feeling strange and out of place. It no longer felt scary or strange to me at all. *I know this is your way of reminding me that my life is in your hands, God. I give it all up to you. I am yours.*

That spring, I began praying for a wife to help me raise my boys. "God, I love my mother, but I can't live with her forever. Please bring a good woman into my life."

Just be Chris, I felt God say to me. *Follow me, pray to me and honor me.*

And so I did just that, trusting in God, trying to honor him. I believed he'd bring me the right woman in his perfect timing.

Our friends who'd helped us move out to Lebanon had a teenage daughter, Wendy, who worked at a local restaurant. One day, I asked her, "Hey, do you have any friends who are about 30 years old and looking to get married?"

To my surprise, she said, "I actually do have a friend your age. You would like her. Her name's Mandy. I'll tell her about you."

I worked up the courage to call Mandy at the restaurant one day. "I heard you're single. I know this sounds weird, but I was wondering if you'd want to go out on a date sometime with me?"

Mandy politely declined. "Sorry I wasted your time," I mumbled, hanging up. I felt disappointed but was determined not to give up.

I contacted Wendy and told her what had happened with Mandy. "I looked like a fool!" I said.

"I'm so sorry. I forgot to tell her about you. I promise I will," Wendy said.

A week after Easter, I called Mandy again. "I'd like to meet you face to face," I told her.

"Sometimes we close shop at 2 p.m.," she said. "You could come in the restaurant afterward, and we could talk."

I was working part-time at a pizza place. The guys I worked with made a heart-shaped pizza, and I brought it to Mandy on our first date. We hit it off right away, talking for hours. For our second date, we went out for Mexican food. Mandy had all the qualities I was looking for in a woman — kindhearted, funny, with a love for God and a great smile, too. Like me, she was a single parent and was trying to raise a young daughter on her own. *God, is this the woman for me?* I prayed after our date. *I could really see a future with her.*

Be honest, I felt God say. *Tell her who you are.*

"I like you a lot," I told Mandy. "I'm a single dad with two young boys at home. I'm really looking for someone to come alongside me and help raise them."

Mandy's eyes welled with tears. "I've been praying for the same thing for seven years," she said. "I've been asking God to bring me a man to help me raise my daughter."

At that moment, I felt certain it was meant to be. Mandy and I were the answer to each other's prayers. *God was surely in this.*

Slowly, God showed me the areas I needed to work on. On Mother's Day that May, I decided to get drunk. I had a pack of cigarettes with me, as well as a cigar and a joint. As I sat outside, drinking beer and looking up at the stars, I felt God say to me, *This woman has standards much higher than yours. The things you are doing need to stop.*

You're right, God. Mandy is a gift, and I don't want to lose her. I don't need this stuff anymore. Right then and there, I stopped doing everything. I threw it all in the dumpster and walked away. This surely was the power of God in me, because I know I could not have done it on my own. I'd been a slave to drugs and booze since my youth, and despite trying to stop many times, I'd never fully kicked my destructive habits. But with God on my side, he gave me the strength to make better choices. I desired to live for him now, not myself.

As I walked away that afternoon, I felt as though he smiled down on me, saying to me, *I've got you, Chris. You're going to be okay.*

By that summer, Mandy and I began discussing marriage. We bought rings and licenses and made plans. But I began getting nervous, realizing I'd have to ask my mother to leave my house.

One September day, I went to Mandy's restaurant, and she fed me some breakfast. The eggs were soggy, and I sensed her growing impatient as we sat there and talked.

"Chris, are you going to marry me or not?" she demanded, half laughing.

I called a pastor, and he agreed to marry us that very

day. We wed in a simple ceremony with our mothers and children present. It was a beautiful moment I'll never forget as long as I live. Nothing had ever felt so right.

I began going to Mandy's church and started getting involved. We enjoyed newlywed life, merging our families together. Knowing I didn't want to work retail and fast food forever, I prayed about finding a better job. Mandy's aunt suggested I look in the newspaper. I found a job opening for a bank teller supervisor but laughed off the idea. *I'm a high school dropout and a former drug user. Who would want to hire me?*

One day, during prayer at church, I felt God nudging me. *Go apply for that job.*

I marched down to the bank. It took me an hour and a half to fill out the application. The secretary thanked me as I handed it to her and began to walk away. "You have a good day," she said.

Turn around and ask her a question, I felt God say.

I turned around. "When will the position be filled?" I asked.

Moments later, I found myself on an unofficial interview. I answered each question truthfully, not mincing words. *God will take care of me,* I reminded myself.

"Have you ever made mistakes at your previous jobs?" the woman asked.

"I have, and I will continue to make mistakes," I answered truthfully. "But I have become wiser through my mistakes and learned what not to do."

The woman smiled when we'd finished. "I really like you," she said.

I landed the job.

For a while, it seemed like the perfect fit. But eventually, I realized it was time for me to move on. I took the situation to God, asking him to give me wisdom. My boss left to work at her father's company, and she called one day to ask if I'd like to come on board. I accepted the offer, thanking God for answering my prayer. He continued to take care of me and my new family, providing for us above and beyond. I knew I could always trust in him.

࿇࿇࿇

After some big changes at our church, Mandy and I felt God leading us on to LifePoint Church in Lebanon. We immediately fell in love with the warm people, the youth group and the pastor.

When Mandy gave birth to our beautiful little daughter Amy she completed our wonderful family. My boys are both thriving students and athletes, and Mandy's daughter is active in choir and a top student as well. I could not be more proud of them all.

"I am not saying I have it all together, that I have it made. But I am well on my way, reaching out for Christ, who has so wondrously reached out for me," I told my church friends one week. "Friends, don't get me wrong. By no means do I count myself an expert on all this. But I've got my eye on the goal — Jesus. I'm off and running, and I'm not turning back."

Years ago, I was a lying, stealing, promiscuous meth addict. In the trenches, I saw no hope for my future. I reached my lowest point, feeling alone, tired and afraid. But Jesus pulled me out of that pit. He was my lifeline, and when I clung to him, he rescued me.

I am proof that God can use anyone, no matter how dirty or mucked up he or she might be. Since clinging to him, I have found an unexplainable peace. I learned to trust him for each aspect of my life, and he has always provided. He has breathed life into me, letting me begin again. And I can't wait to keep moving forward with him.

CONCLUSION

When I first read these stories, my eyes filled with tears because these are people I know and love. I've been so blessed to walk with them through these challenges and to help them find their healing. It's been exciting to see their lives transform at every level. As I often say, nothing's better than ringside seats to life change!

I celebrate what God's done in the lives of these brave men and women and am so humbled that they were willing to share their stories to help encourage and inspire others. But I confess that my heart is still heavy because so many people still struggle, still believe their lives will remain forever broken.

Here at LifePoint, we exist for the singular purpose of pointing everyone to a deeper, more meaningful life by connecting people to Christ and to each other. Perhaps you noticed that in every story in this book, God did an amazing work in someone's life, and he worked *through another person* in some way. In fact, that's how you got this book. It wasn't by accident. We believe God put it on someone's heart to put this book in your hands. No matter who you are — man or woman; young or old; white collar, blue collar or no collar; city slicker, suburbanite, redneck or Ozark hillbilly — and regardless of how you might classify yourself, we believe God loves you so much, he gave his son to save you.

You might need to read that last line again.

God *loves* you. God loves *you*.

God loves you *so much*, he gave his son to save you.

To save YOU.

What do you do with a statement like that?

If you are like me, maybe there's been a moment in your life when you thought, *God might love a lot of people, just not me.* You may have thought, *No way God could ever really love me, not like I am now. There are things I need to change first.* It is common for us to think that, but I believe it couldn't be further from the truth.

Maybe your pain is the "proof" you use to convince yourself that God isn't real. Perhaps you're angry over the very idea of God loving anyone, especially yourself.

Or maybe you have heard that line so many times, it just falls flat with you.

I can't speak to all of the specifics of your experience, but I can assure you that God's word tells us that God loves us just like we are.

The Apostle Paul addresses this very idea in a letter he penned to the church in Rome when he wrote that "God demonstrates his own love for us in this: While we were still sinners, Christ died for us" (Romans 5:8). In other words, God loved us *before* we loved him, with all our flaws, even when we held contempt for him in our hearts. His love for us is there before we ever change a single thing.

The reason I write about God's love in a book like this is because it's the one constant that all these stories share.

God's love is and always will be the single most powerful catalyst to life change we can experience.

Even as I write this, I know some people feel so far away from God and his love that they struggle to believe it is real. I get that. There was a time when I personally struggled to believe that God could love me "warts and all." It seems many people believe that if we want God to love us or to change our situation, we first need to fix all our issues, stop all our bad behaviors or get our act together — and then, after all of that, maybe God would look on us with compassion.

But what I discovered, and what I hope you begin to understand, is that God's love isn't conditional. He loves us. And all our efforts to change, successful or otherwise, do not change that. God could not love you less, and he could not love you more. He simply loves you. Period.

But God's love alone isn't enough to change us. We must embrace that love and accept it for ourselves, and that is when things start to happen. If you would like to see what changes God can make in your life, first accept his love. Then let God help you follow these next steps:

- Admit you need God and his help and power in your life.
- Believe that Jesus Christ alone can save you from your sins.
- Confess all your sins to God, and ask God to forgive you.
- Dedicate yourself to living according to God's standards from this moment on.

None of this is rocket science. The Apostle Paul wrote that if you will simply "Declare with your mouth, 'Jesus is Lord,' and believe in your heart that God raised him from the dead, you will be saved" (Romans 10:9). If you are ready to do these four things, why not take some time to pray to God right now? Here is a simple prayer you could use:

Lord Jesus, I know that I don't have all the answers, and I have made many mistakes in my life that have left my life broken. But as I read about how you love me and how you have the power to change lives, I ask you to save me from all the wrong things I have done. I regret those decisions and now am ready to live life according to your ways. I believe you died and rose again in order to set me free, and now I ask you to be the Lord of my life and the forgiver of my sins. Please change me, Lord, that my life may be unbroken for you. Give me the strength and wisdom I need, and help me to know when you are guiding me. Thank you for everything you have done to save and change me. Amen.

If you prayed that prayer and believe these things in your heart, then congratulations! The process of authentic life change has begun!

And now that you have taken these steps, here are a few more that would be wise for you to take:

CONCLUSION

Get plugged into a church.

Christians are meant to do life together. The Bible tells us in Hebrews 10:25, "Let us not neglect our meeting together, as some people do, but encourage one another, especially now that the day of his return is drawing near" (NLT). We need to be in relationship with fellow believers so that we are able to get encouragement, accountability and support for when life's troubles happen. If you don't already have a church, we would love for you to join us here at LifePoint. We are a group of imperfect people seeking God's direction for our lives. We invite you to join us, bring your questions and we will walk together to find the answers.

If you do have a church, then by all means, go talk to your pastor about getting connected even more for greater growth.

Get plugged into the Bible.

The Bible is God's love letter to us, given to teach us about God and guide us into living lives that are pleasing to him. If you want to know how God would lead you to live your life, look to his word. The psalmist writes, "Your word is a lamp unto my feet and a light unto my path" (Psalm 119:105). God's word provides us with the direction we need as we walk down the paths of life. If you don't have a Bible that you can read and easily understand, LifePoint would be happy to give you one. Just stop by or contact us, and we will put one in your hand!

We're delighted to share these stories with you. We believe God's story is still unfolding here in the Ozarks and that God's calling you to participate. Don't be afraid. He is a God worth trusting. I hope to see you soon!

Grace and Peace,

Kelly Rhoades
Lead Pastor
LifePoint Church
Lebanon, Missouri

We would love for you to join us at
LifePoint Church!

We meet Sunday mornings at 8:30, 10 and 11:30 a.m.
and Wednesdays at 5:45 p.m. at
195 N. Washington Avenue, Lebanon, MO 65536.

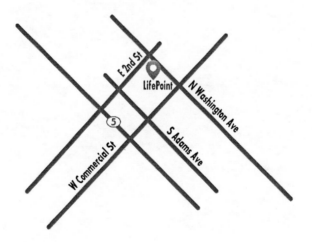

Contact us at 417.991.2911 or at
www.lifepointlebanon.com.